This book is dedicated to Robin Williams, who I never knew but understood. Rest in peace.

1951-2014

carpe diem

This book is family friendly and contains no vulgarity, sex or violence.

May God bless you with peace and love.

The greatest is love.

John: 3:16

To God be the Glory

Edited by Anne E. Bauswein

Printed in the USA by DiggyPOD

Copyright © 2014 Nicholas D. Timcisko

ISBN: 978-1-63315-516-9

Disclaimer

The names in this book are real and the observations my own. This is a book of facts, opinions and truth. There is some embellishment but I present things as I saw them. What you get are observations through the eyes of a man who suffers within double vision since a childhood eye injury.

You probably will experience a broad spectrum of feelings and thoughts because this is a story about life; how it was and how many wish it were.

If you are too young to understand some of the terms, buy a good dictionary and look them up. Have fun as we journey through life together.

A laugh, smile, frown or tear along the way is normal. A smile is better for your face.

Forgive me if I missed anyone as I tell the story. I'll include you in the next book.

Dedication

This is dedicated to Carol, our children, Lori, Scott and Tiffany; grandchildren, Kayla, Tyler, Jennifer, Julia, Nicholas, Matthew, Sophia and Maria.

The men in my life: Ed Wasko, Dom Monaco, Carmen Julius, Carmen Lanzo (Jane), James R. Lanzo (Kristine), Dr. Dumitru Teodorescu, Pastor Len Evans (Betty), Pastor Joe Mazzu (Charlotte), Jack Smith, Father Paul Vasko, Father Mike Scanlon and my brother, Jon Ricky.

The key women: Sophia Wasko, Cecelia Wasko (Timcisko), Carol Dill, Amelia Dill (Earl), Linda Fiorelli (Bob) and Martha "Martie" Graban.

Music is still a big part of my life. Thank you to the Del Rays: Joe "Mouse" Kalaman, Bruce Dill (Patty), Danny Carbon (Sharon); Joe "Pappy" Kalaman (Mary), Tony Klepec (Ann) and Stan Kenton.

I thank God and Jesus Christ, my savior, for life. I am indebted to Reverend Billy Graham for showing me "The Way." My helper is the Holy Spirit.

I challenge you to become better, one day at a time. Vince Lombardi said, "Give thanks to God, your family and the Green Bay Packers [work]."

Prologue

"Tomorrow, and tomorrow, and tomorrow. The days creep slowly along until the end of time."

Shakespeare's Macbeth (Modern Text)

I am a project starter. Finishing was the challenge. I planned to write a book, screenplay, song, learn to read music, play guitar, piano and keyboard. I'll bet you understand and know how it goes.

Thought with no action results in nothing. Thought with half action equals work but still nothing. My escapes were, later (finish it later) and tomorrow (things will get better tomorrow). I lived my life like many others in Later Land and Tomorrow Land.

I've always been a dreamer, but I became a planner. My weak points: lousy implementer, bad at follow through and a weak finisher. Can you relate?

The idea for this book entered my mind after right hip replacement surgery in 2001. I combined the original idea with another after my left hip was replaced in 2009. I guess this makes the book "hip."

I begin to diligently write in the middle of 2013.

Foreword

Life is built on the foundation of experience, strengthened by education and love. Here is a good way to start each day.

1. In all things be on time. Fifteen minutes early is better.

2. Give your employer more than what your pay requires.

3. Always be honest, truthful, trustworthy and forgiving.

4. Love, unconditionally, expecting nothing in return.

5. Develop a relationship with a higher power.

With these actions you can build a solid foundation and develop a reputation. Remember, you never get a second chance to make a first impression.

This book is for anyone. You'll find much to ponder when you read about the experiences, endeavors and attitudes molded over seventy years. You will relate to success, failure, highs, lows and challenges.

I love people and live with a positive attitude as a committed Christian, not perfect but being perfected. It wasn't always this way. By faith, I know where I will spend eternity.

Contents

Disclaimer

Dedication

Prologue

Forward

Title	Chapter	Page
Beginning	1	9
Music Starts	2	31
Work & School	3	49
Xerox	4	63
Ohio	5	81
The Cigar Shop	6	92
Roaming	7	132
Photos and Music	8	146
Hawaii	9	160
Finish	10	178
A Message		181
After Thoughts		184
About the Author		186

Beginning

Years ago I started referring to myself as the illegitimate son of Jonathan Winters, the great American comedian who battled mental illness. I bare an uncanny resemblance to him and have mental problems. I never knew my real father so only God knows the truth.

My maternal grandmother, Sophia, married Stephan Wasko, a popular Slovak man and a drinker. They had five children and he abandoned them. I was told he went to California looking for gold.

Grandma was short, frail but strong. She had no formal education and spoke broken English. Maybe you can understand since many of your relatives may have been immigrants.

Sophie came to this country from Czechoslovakia, today the Czech Republic and Slovakia. She was a hard worker, a devout Roman Catholic and independent. She raised her five children with no support from her spouse and she raised me.

I believed everything she said but didn't always understand her. Grandma was a saint. I hope you were lucky enough to know someone like her.

When I was a baby, my Uncle Ed, home from the US Air Force, saved my life. I fell from my crib onto a broken glass. He ran with me in his arms to our family physician. I have a scar ending above my left eye. It is a constant reminder of how blessed and protected by God I have been.

Like many, I lost contact with aunts, uncles, cousins and went my own way. I enjoyed my relationships with them and they are forever in my memory.

Everyone has a favorite uncle and Ed, Grandma's oldest son, was mine. In World War II, many young men quit school and joined the service. After thirty years in the Air Force, he retired, and like many soldiers never talked about what he did. The family thought it had to do with Intelligence because he had a top secret clearance.

Ed loved to walk but rarely owned a car. He had a girlfriend in Germany, never married and traveled the world. He was my inspiration. People admired him because he was a self-made man.

His library included a collection of literature and philosophy. He loved art, music and history, and spoke English, Slovak, French, Italian, German and Spanish. He had a beautiful block style of handwriting and always wrote with a fountain pen.

In 1982 Ed died mysteriously while exploring the Mayan Ruins in Mexico. The death was suspicious and his body was finally returned to the United States. He wanted to be buried in the Arlington

National Cemetery but left no will. Today, he is next to his mother and near his brother, Tommy, in St. John's Cemetery, Villa Maria, Ohio.

Everyone has a family member like Aunt Clara, who was the lynchpin. She was a generous person who worked at the Record Rendezvous, waitressed at the Hot Dog Shoppe and was a working mother. Once I saw a photo of her in a Hollywood magazine.

She married Steve Berdis, a skilled steelmaker, great athlete and bar owner. He was outgoing, fun loving, played semi-pro baseball and was the life of the party but rough around the edges.

When I visited their home on the West Side, we rode bikes to the Steel Street Cafe. There were always free pop and snacks. The mills ran three shifts: 7-3 (day) 3-11 (afternoon) and 11-7 (night). Many steelworkers drank after work to unwind because the mill was stressful and dangerous.

A favorite drink was the "boilermaker," a shot of whisky with a glass of beer. Taverns had pickled eggs in a jar and sandwiches. Penny machines dispensed peanuts and everyone played the "bug," a type of gambling. Paychecks were cashed and shuffleboard and pin-ball machines were always busy. It was the era of cash only.

You may be old enough to recall going to a local poultry store to buy a live chicken. The bird would be killed, plucked, cleaned, butchered and cooked, usually on Sunday at the family dinner after church. It was a weekly ritual.

Remember when everything had a time and place? Monday was wash day and garments were hung on a clothesline secured by wooden clothes pins and dried by the sun.

Cleaning and vacuuming were done on Friday. The mills spewed smoke and soot and there was no Environmental Protection Agency to control pollution. Times were booming and the air was dirty and smelly in a town with heavy industry.

Auntie's home had a parlor, uncommon in those days, and a store front where we played. There was the fruit cellar, a room dug into the earth which was always cool, damp and musty. It's where canned vegetables from the garden were stored.

My mother, Cecelia Delores Wasko, was attractive and outgoing. She loved to dance and made friends easily. In 1943, she became pregnant with me but wasn't married. I arrived early (premature) and there was a high probability I would die but I made it into the world. God had a plan.

Her friend Harry an excellent dancer, became a state senator. Shy, a well-known local musician owned a tailor shop. All of my pants as a boy were custom made and I may have unknowingly met my real father because there was never a charge. He ran ads that said, "Don't be shy, see Shy for clothing."

Jim, a city bus driver, would often transport us to town at no charge. A weekly bus pass was usually controlled by a person like Mrs. Merva, who would lend you hers if you intended to go to town. You'd borrow and return it when you were done. If you needed extra luggage you asked around.

Did your town have a popular department store? Youngstown had Strouss-Hirshberg Company. In the basement was a shop that sold "Frosted Malteds." They were cold, smooth and tasty. Think of pudding. The only flavor was chocolate and they were better than a Wendy's Frosty. The machines are still in use somewhere in the area.

The store featured a restaurant and grill on the ground floor and served the tastiest hamburgers on a toasted bun. One of their nicest employees, an openly gay fellow, was kind and well liked but people made fun of him because he had a strange haircut.

The Italian restaurant across the street served great chili con-carne and fresh baked Italian bread. It was dimly lit and had character. Placed on every table were two large shakers with slits instead of holes. One had pepper seeds, the other parmesan cheese and when you dispensed the contents, plenty flowed onto your delicious meal.

Mother was an opinionated Democrat and active in politics. She believed Democrats were for the poor and Republicans for the wealthy.

I didn't know what a Republican was until I was in my forties and the last Democrat to get my vote was Jimmy Carter. Change is constant and I changed. Today, I wonder if it matters since things seem corrupt and out of balance.

I've always been conservative but liberal regarding social issues. Because of my birth, I couldn't endorse abortion and always supported adoption. I know abstinence is difficult but it minimizes issues and problems. Other than my mother and grandmother, there has only been one other woman in my life, my wife Carol. It's not impossible to control yourself.

Uncle Tom was a hardened man. He was a paratrooper with the 101st Airborne "Screaming Eagles." During the last battle of World War II in Germany, he was wounded.

He had an attitude, didn't like people gawking at him and was a man of few words. The back fender of his Harley Davidson motorcycle was draped with fancy leather saddlebags and he smoked big cigars.

Like many veterans returning from the war Tommy worked at the Youngstown Sheet and Tube, a steel mill. I was careful when I asked him anything because I was afraid of him.

One day in the middle of a week, he announced "I'm getting married on Saturday." Grandma was shocked and didn't attend the wedding. Mary was Greek Orthodox not Roman Catholic and the ceremony was at her church. Sophie slowly grew to love her.

Uncle Jimmy, her youngest son, was handsome and a free spirit. He joined the Navy and I don't think he was ever without a chew (Copenhagen) in his mouth. During the war, he served on battleships. The last one was referred to as Battleship X. Women fawned over him and he was a smooth talker.

He became a union representative in the mill and married a girl from West Virginia. He eventually retired but was forever bitter toward management like many steel workers in Northeast Ohio. It was a blue collar area where management was the enemy.

In my early my teens, I had an accident that almost destroyed my right eye. My brother, Jon, and friend, Johnny, were playing in Pine Hollow, a wooded area with a deep gorge filled with rocks and wild growth. There is a creek flowing through the middle and a pool at one end deep enough to take a dip.

Remote places like Dead Man's cave was a place to play. The opening was narrow and a natural spring flowed from the rocky wall. Someone drove a pipe into the source and cold water constantly poured out the end. We drank fresh water from the pipe.

We were running fast when I stopped and turned. Johnny plowed into me, knocking me out. I came to in a daze and ordered my companions to go home and not tell anyone. I was dizzy and scared.

Home was only a few miles away but I couldn't keep my balance and crawled on my hands and knees. A man stopped his car and asked if I was sick. He drove me to the top of my street but I wouldn't allow him to go further. I knew something bad happened. I felt strange and the normally short walk had taken four hours even with a ride.

I climbed the stairs to the bathroom and when I looked in the mirror, the right side of my face was badly swollen and my right eye was positioned in the upper corner of the socket. I took a bath and tried to hide.

When mother saw me she almost fainted and took me to a prominent eye surgeon. He said every muscle that controlled my right eye was damaged and I would need surgery. Unfortunately, there was one muscle that could not be repaired.

I have permanent double vision and compensate by adjusting my head to see one image. It kept me out of Vietnam where two of my best friends were killed. Thank you for serving if you were there.

If you grew up in a small town like Campbell, where I lived until I was 21 years old, it was a treat. I spent most of my youth with Grandma Wasko. She lived on the second floor of a tenement house at 101 Gordon Avenue. The Gordon Elementary School was across the street. I lived there as a baby with my unmarried mother and spent most of my youth with grandma because she lived alone.

The neighborhood was cosmopolitan: Eastern Europeans from Czechoslovakia, Croatia, Serbia, Ukraine, Hungary and Yugoslavia, as well as Italians from Naples, Calabria, Rome and Greeks from every part of Greece.

Blacks and Latinos were referred to as "colored people" and many were from the South. At one time there was an influx of Puerto Ricans. We all played together and were friends.

Her five-room place faced the steel mill. She never owned a car and a city bus took her everywhere. It was a small universe.

Like most apartments you were not permitted to have a live pet so I had a rubber dog named Poochie. He was brown with big floppy ears and I would play with him for hours. I took old socks, cut off the ends and made hats. Clothes were created out of the middle of the sock and he had a bed.

Today, I keep him on display in my office and take him on vacations.

Everyone has a best friend and Jim, whose family was Italian, lived a block away with his mother, father and brother, Carmen, who was fifteen years older. There was also Uncle Dave, "Duke" James, Aunt Rosie and his grandfather who we called "Papoo." His home was constantly filled with people.

There was always a big selection of food on the large dinner table: spaghetti, meatballs, salad, desserts and Jell-O. Uncle Jim would say, "There's always room for Jell-O." Jimmy's backyard overlooked the city dump where we played.

In simpler times, the radio was constantly tuned to Cleveland Indians baseball. We made score cards and diagramed every game as we listened to Jimmy Dudley announce the play by play. "The string is out" (when it was a full count), and the ball is "going, going, gone!" (a home run) were his trademark sayings.

Did you ever wake up in the summer and run to somewhere like Gordon School to play baseball? Wooden bats were held together by nails and black tape rolled around a broken handle.

Baseballs were covered with electrical tape and more oval than round. Occasionally we got a new unbroken bat and a real baseball. That was special.

18

Leather baseball gloves were hand me downs and well used. We kept them soaked with "Neatsfoot" leather oil.

Pick-up games started when guys showed up. You were selected to play and teams expanded as others arrived. Each team usually ended up with nine players. Without a full team, we modified the rules. Right field might be an automatic out. When you stepped on the pitcher's mound before the runner reached first base, he was out.

Everyone dreamed of making it to the major leagues and our Cleveland Indians heroes were outfielder Rocky Colovito, catcher Jim Hegan, third baseman Al Rosen and future Hall of Fame pitcher Bob "Rapid Robert" Feller. We learned to chew "Browns Mule" plug chewing tobacco. It made me sick.

We all played sports yet there was no socializing or sleepovers and we kept to ourselves. Almost everyone had a family with a mother and father and attended a church.

I was adopted and didn't talk about it. Anger and depression built up in me. I rarely spoke about divorce because I was ashamed. I never said I had a step-father or step-brother, Jon Ricky.

The family home on 112 Regent Street was owned by my adopted grandparents, Michael and Anna. It had three bedrooms and one bath so sharing and waiting was the norm. Grandpa Mike installed a shower in the cellar which helped.

The house was old and I hated the wet basement which smelled musty because of a cracked foundation. For storage there was a wooden ice box.

Four adults and two children made the two story house crowded. I technically lived there and had to attend Reed School.

The Campbell school system was made up of Memorial High School, Reed, Gordon, Penhale and McCartney grade schools and the Board of Education building. Today, progress has destroyed these structures. Back in the day students walked everywhere, including school.

I had my own bedroom at Grandma's and immediate access to the bathroom which was in a hall. You had to turn on the gas and light the burner to heat water. After ten minutes you could bathe.

Does you remember the huge porcelain bathtubs with claw feet where clothes were cleaned using a washboard? Fels Naphtha, a disinfectant soap that smelled pungent, was rubbed into the garments. I still use that soap. Wouldn't you like to have the tub?

One day Grandma moved to the third floor and I thought we were moving up. The reason was lower rent. Grandma made little money and barely survived.

Her son, Ed, who made a career of the Air Force, sent money every month for her to live. She was poor but wouldn't take welfare, then called relief. Now I had additional stairs to climb but a better view of the smoky mill and city dump. For me, it was a happy day.

She loved me and shielded me from many things. "There was nobody like her, Nicky," my aunt Clara used to say. She was the best person in my life. I know many of you can relate.

Grandma loved movies and the Bell Theater was a ten-minute walk. We went to nearly every show and saw the classics. It cost ten cents for her and a nickel for me. Popcorn came in a box that I converted to fake binoculars after the hot tasty product was eaten. Candy was a penny and candy bars five cents.

You watched a newsreel, then the previews of coming attractions which gave you a look at future movies and at least one cartoon before the feature. There were special Saturdays with only cartoons and all the neighborhood kids would show up.

Most films were black and white and there were the serials: Flash Gordon, The Little Rascals, Sky King and many more. They were short and closed without a final ending so you had to return the following week to see what happened next.

Theaters had special events like "bank night" when you got a ticket and won money if your number was drawn. Charities like the March of Dimes collected for their organizations. We'd put in a few pennies and a dime was a good donation.

I attended grade school from kindergarten through the seventh grade. I was in love with Miss James, my kindergarten teacher. Mr. Gould, the principal, was a disciplinarian and Mr. Grazinski, the vice-principal, was kind. Mr. Buccilli taught woodworking which I took in the sixth and seventh grade. He was cool and I related to him. Today, I still use the skills we learned and have a cutting board I made in 1957.

Mr. Cvengros taught English. He was challenging and demanding, and I respected him. Years later, he attended my wedding. Mr. Monaco, the guidance counselor, was a gentle, soft-spoken man who everyone loved. Most of the teachers were great.

Nearly every boy began each summer with a pair of white US Keds, high-top basketball shoes. We stuffed cardboard in the soles when they wore out and by summer's end they were smelly and shot. It was a time when you saved everything and found a use for junk.

A favorite activity centered on nails. We recycled old nails by pounding them straight with a hammer. Reusing them more than once was normal. We'd go to a nearby building site to search for dropped nails. It was like searching for treasure. Straight, unused virgin nails were a delicacy, as they say in the world of fine food.

The Dairy Queen was a local hang out. On most evenings during summer we would play "buck-buck." It was a game played by two teams. One of the bigger boys called the post would lean against a brick wall. The next player called a horse would bend over and wedge his shoulder into the post. Each succeeding player (horse) would bend over and place his head under the previous person's butt and form a line. If a guy farted he was razzed. Imagine a line of boys bent over with their heads under each other's rear end leaning against one guy. This was team one.

The members of the second team would run as fast as possible and leap onto the back of the horses. Each member of the opposing team got as close to the post as possible without falling off. You hung on to a horse. The next boy would run, leap and hang on.

If the horses collapsed, the team leaping got to do it again. If the line didn't collapse and a member of the jumping team didn't fall off, the post would shout "buck-buck, how many fingers up?" and hold up fingers.

One of the bent over horses would guess a number. If it was correct or a member of the leaping team fell, the other team got a turn. We played for hours. It was physically back breaking and our idea of fun.

Every kid with any ambition during my youth had a newspaper delivery route. Our local paper, *The Youngstown Vindicator*, was a daily and if the local manager liked you, a route was to be had. Generally a route covered 50 to 100 subscribers. Papers were dropped at a street location in bundles. Every carrier had a cloth newspaper bag which was used to carry and deliver the papers. Papers had to be folded to fit neatly in the bag and folding the daily paper was an art that we had to learn as the size (thickness) of the newspaper varied from day to day. The daily was tossed onto the driveway or porch but we always had customers who wanted their paper placed in a mailbox or some other specific location. Saturday was usually collection day.

On Sunday, there was always a second bundle with the ads and it was our job to collate the two bundles. The Sunday edition was always multi-sectioned and thick. All paper boys had a wagon to transport the Sunday edition which was the largest edition in the week. On most Sundays we'd congregate at our stop and race our wagons down a big hill.

Besides delivering the paper, collecting the money and being on time, we were expected to get new subscribers by cold calling people who didn't get the paper. Some patrons only got the Sunday edition.

Good services usually resulted in tips. A little extra coin was a big help in those days. One of my best customers, Pete, lived on the second floor of an apartment. He wanted the paper placed at his doorstep and always gave me a large tip every week for my inconvenience. It was worth the extra effort.

Christmas was special. Most customers usually wrote a Christmas card to me and included a bonus which they presented on collection day. I had a few taverns and businesses on my route which provided eats, soft drinks and more around the holiday.

When I played football I'd hire my friend Stanley to cover my route. I learned about subcontracting. After a few years I handed the route over to my friend Larry who recently reconnected with me after 53 years.

What is your favorite sport? I loved football. When you graduated from seventh grade you went to Memorial High, a basic brick structure. Behind it was a beautiful football stadium built by the WPA during President Roosevelt's administration.

Our city park was named Roosevelt Park in his honor and I bet you had something in your town named after him. Football was king of sports in the Steel Valley. A large portion of the city tax was paid by the mills and the Red Devils, for a small school, had a powerful well-funded football team.

Five good friends I knew or played football with became big time athletes. Bob Babich, played for the San Diego Chargers and Cleveland Browns in the NFL. Larry Carwell became a star at Iowa. Andy Cverko played for the Dallas Texans, coached by legendary Tom Landry. In his autobiography, Landry talks about him.

When I started high school, Andy and his younger brother Jack were great players. During the summer I would train with them. Both were smart and earned scholarships to Northwestern University, a fine engineering school. They became football and academic All-Americans.

Albert "Abe" Gerlick played for Syracuse. Our team made a trip to Pittsburgh to see the Orange Men, coached by Ben Schwartzwalder, play the Pitt Panthers. Naturally, our focus was on Al, a former Memorial Red Devil. He kicked field goals.

His teammate was the great running back Ernie Davis, the first African-American to win the Heisman Trophy. We saw a lot more of Ernie. After the game we met Al on the muddy field. He was our hero. Ernie, the first draft pick of the Cleveland Browns, died of leukemia before the season started.

We all know that life has its disappointments. I loved to make contact and was scheduled to be the starting offensive left guard and defensive middle guard as a junior. I was five foot five, one hundred seventy-five pounds. In small schools you often played both ways.

Frank, a six foot tall, three hundred pound giant decided to try out for football. Head coach Johnny Knapic was enamored with him. This kid could do damage in the middle because he was huge.

Defensive coach Carmen Julius wanted me to start but Frank was big and Knapic chose him. Naturally, I was upset as I expected to play both ways. He lasted only a few downs because he wasn't mobile, and I got my starting position on defense.

We didn't have a good year and football ended when I graduated. A family friend wanted me to try out for Oklahoma, a college powerhouse coached by Bud Wilkinson. I knew I was too small and passed on the opportunity.

Years later I attended a party and spoke to Jimmy who played my left guard spot after I graduated. He was an excellent player and told my wife that in his opinion, I was one of the best middle guards he ever saw. I beamed when he said, "If Nick were taller he'd be playing in the NFL." Thanks, Jimmy, but probably not!

Many of us spent our youth visiting other neighborhoods. Campbell had section I often visited. These articles from the 2012 and 2013 *Vindicator* tell the story well.

"In just a few days, the Iron Soup Historical Preservation Co. will open its fourth fully restored unit to its new tenants.

Located at 56 Chambers St., the one-bedroom, two-story unit built by the Youngstown Sheet & Tube Co. isn't much more than 600 square feet. It's also nearing the one-century mark.

But as Tim Sokoloff, the preservation company's president and chairman, explained, the 179 remaining concrete units in the six-acre complex of row houses are still as sturdy today as they were back in 1918 — despite years of damage caused by vagrants and vandals.

This was the first modern apartment complex ever built on the planet. It used to be a beautiful place to live.

The units were built after a Youngstown Sheet & Tube Co. strike, during which workers protested poor living conditions and wages.

In an effort to appease those workers, the company ensured that each unit came equipped with practically every modern convenience of the era: hot and cold running water, gas and electric.

There was a storage/utility room below each unit that was accessed by walking out the back door and down a short flight of steps.

At the time, most of these amenities were available only to the wealthy and elite — but were provided to the average Youngstown Sheet & Tube Co. employee who lived in the complex.

The complex was also innovative in its construction. Pre-fabricated concrete slabs were assembled with cranes, marking one of the earliest uses of concrete for domestic architecture.

"It's simply a monumental site," Sokoloff said, "which is why Iron Soup has made it its mission to preserve and revitalize the units and, to a greater extent, the neighborhood."

At 56 Chambers St., for example, the unit still retained its electric and plumbing, along with fixtures including its bathtub and kitchen cabinets. Of Iron Soup's units, it was the "closest one to get up and running," Sokoloff said, and has taken about three weeks to restore.

For more information about the Iron Soup Historical Preservation Co., which is headquartered at 40 Chambers Street, Campbell, Ohio and its mission, visit www.ironsoup.com.

"The leader of a group that works to restore the Sheet & Tube company homes says it's time for Campbell leaders to take more interest in the homes.

The group owns 19 of the 179 homes that are left in the complex, which consists of one- and two-unit apartments in concrete row houses that were the first of their kind. They were built for people who worked in the Campbell plant. They are on the National Register of Historic Places.

When I returned to college, my grandmother lived in one of these homes until she died. 293 Robinson Road is one of the houses in disrepair. I hope to get involved in this project and may restore the place. I have many fond memories of this area where many of my boyhood friends were raised.

Music Starts

At one time or another, most of us dream of fame and fortune. How many times did you think of being someone famous when you were a kid? We all have engaged in the game, "Let's pretend."

I love listening to music and singing. I did my first solo in the third grade during a program for the PTA and sang the "The Peace Pipe Song."

Thinking about the 1950s, you may remember a change in music as the big band era started to end. Pop music was maturing. "The" song in 1956 was "In the Still of the Night" by the Five Satins. Our boys' bathroom had marble walls and was the perfect place to vocalize. It was the song we sang most.

My classmates, Kenny, Steve and Earl would meet and sing the songs of the day in harmony. The 1960s started the Doo-Wop era. Rock & Roll was here to stay. The Beatles and the British invasion changed everything.

Eighth graders at Memorial High were called "greenies," and abused by upper class students. When you asked for help, you were sure to be sent in the wrong direction. We were treated like vermin, got by and learned the ropes. The next year we hassled the new greenies.

On Fridays, all classes reported to the auditorium for an assembly. The school population was small so everyone was seated. We'd hear a speech, watch a play and sometime there was music.

One particular assembly featured a local singing group, The Edsels: brothers Larry and Harry, James, nicknamed "Pee Wee," Marshall, and George. They graduated from Campbell and were well known. Backed by a live band, they did one of the most exciting shows I ever witnessed. I still talk about the performance.

The five sang beautiful lead and harmony. They moved like gazelles generating energy. A few years later, the recording "Ram-a-Lama Ding Dong" was discovered and became a hit.

They signed with Capitol Records and appeared on Dick Clark's television show, "American Bandstand." Recently I saw them on TV in a Doo-Wop special from Pittsburgh doing their hit song.

Louie came to Memorial from Cleveland. He was a handsome Greek kid, played piano and decided to start a band. Denny, played drums and I became the lead singer. Lou said he was asking Joe, nicknamed "Mouse," to join the combo and I wasn't happy.He always wore black, acted like a juvenile delinquent and was never without his switchblade knife. He played clarinet and saxophone and was good.

Our first rehearsal went well and it turned out that Mouse was nothing like his reputation. His hoodlum demeanor was a mask. We developed a repertoire and booked a few jobs. One of our first was a party at the Pick Ohio Hotel, a beautiful place in downtown Youngstown.

The first song I ever sang for money was Ron Holden's, "Love You So." It was a hit being played on WHOT, the "hot spot," a local AM radio station. You often heard a booming, echoing, "WHOT 1330," announcing the station when they were on the air.

Some of the disc jockeys were "Boots" Bell, Johnny K (Kutan), Dick "DT" Thompson and "GB" George Barry. The station was popular with teens and played the latest rock and roll.

Louie knew the owner of Audio Recording, a studio located in the basement of the WKYC-TV building in Cleveland. We would often travel there and jam with "Tom King and the Starfires" a popular Cleveland band who rehearsed at Audio.

Vlad was a skilled recording engineer with a great ear for sound. Tom played guitar and would allow us to stay when they recorded. He and Louie were good friends. A few years later, they had a national hit "Time Won't Let Me," which they released as The Outsiders. If you listen to oldies, you know it.

The vocalist was Sonny Geraci, a handsome Italian with a beautiful voice. I didn't know Sonny because we stopped visiting the studio. I'd been a professional musician for 25 years when we connected and it had nothing to do with music.

Mouse's father worked for the railroad. Pappy Joe limped because of a war wound, had a handlebar mustache and enjoyed adult beverages. His wife, Mary, was timid. Pappy, a Big Band aficionado, was boss. Mouse spent most of his youth practicing the clarinet and sax. His father had high expectations and intended for him to be the next Benny Goodman, one of the greatest clarinetists. Pappy had a large collection of records, mainly 1940s vintage and music was continually being played. In his opinion it was the only music worth hearing.

Our combo broke up when Louie moved back to Cleveland. Mouse, also played in The Mellow Tones with Aldo, a chubby accordion player and Denny, our drummer. Pappy, a veteran, arranged for the group to play regularly at the VFW club in Struthers. They played standards, polkas and waltzes.

Aldo was leader. His father and Pappy contended for who was boss. They were the transportation since no one was old enough to drive. Mouse invited me to join the band to play guitar and sing. In the late 1950s everyone was playing guitar.

I fooled around with the instrument and had an old Harmony acoustic. I took a few lessons from Tony, a teacher who owned Lucre Music. I wanted to buy a Gretsch white falcon, a beautiful electric guitar but my father said no. I quit after a few lessons and decided to buy a Carvin solid body electric guitar from a company in California. They manufactured a cheap copy of the popular Fender guitar made by Leo Fender and the leader in solid body electric guitars and basses.

My playing in The Mello Tones was fair, so I decided to drill out the tuning heads and put on bass strings. It worked and I started playing electric bass. This was easier because there were only four strings and you didn't play chords which was difficult for me. I had a good ear and could keep a steady beat.

I taught myself to play, purchased an amplifier and began my music career. Today, when people ask, "What do you play?" I reply "for money." I've always been a paid musician. Sometime it wasn't much.

Elmer, Mouse's godfather, owned Pitlik's, a bar on South Avenue. They had live polka music every Friday and Saturday. After the VFW (music ended at 10 p.m.), we'd pack our instruments, pile into our transportation and go to Pitlik's. We played after the regular music was over.

Our pay was free soft drinks and food. Elmer, nicknamed "Pussy," would give us a few bucks. No one outside the VFW ever heard of The Mellow Tones but we got a few weddings when low price was important.

Pappy's brother-in-law lived in Pennsylvania. Elwood City is not far from Youngstown, and each summer the town had an all-day event with music. Mouse's cousin, Dodge, played trombone, his friend Eddie, trumpet, and Terry, the drums. Pappy elected Mouse and me to join them and play. It was a Saturday and we had a brief rehearsal. Dodge and Eddy loved Dixieland music and Mouse and I did anything. After some public appearances, we finished the day playing for a church dance and sounded good for young kids with not much practice. It was a fun day and Dodge and I remained friends. I was at his bedside when he died a few years ago.

The VFW job was steady and one night as we were about to start playing, Mouse announced he was quitting the band to join a rock and roll group. Every teen's dream was to start a rock band and become famous. Maybe you had a garage band.

On the break, he introduced me to his new bandmates. I was mad and whined about how I just got my instrument and lamented, "How could he do this to me?" I'd never be able to get into another

36

band. I sang well but was a mediocre musician. I knew I wouldn't find another group.

Danny and Bruce seemed like fine guys, but to steal Mouse with the intention of starting a new group was beyond me. We had a regular club job that paid and who knew what would develop?

Mouse was always a great musician and said his new friends were very good. My name never entered the discussion as they planned the new band. He suggested the four of us might start a group. I was the weak link musically, but I sang well so we held a rehearsal in his living room. There was a piano which we needed for Danny (before key boards), I'd play bass, Mouse horns and Bruce the drums.

If you were lucky, in the summer you'd get a city job. I worked at the swimming pool. My workmate Jay (not his real name) was a good looking kid who sang. We'd bring our guitars and play on breaks. Our friend Billy, introduced us to barre´ chords, a different method of strumming our well-worn instruments.

Pat, who we called "PW," was the pool manager. He taught high school and was a pushover. As long as the work got done, you were free to do anything within reason and he loved to hear us play and sing. Soon, we were expected to entertain and not work.

His son Doug worked at the pool and arrived with dad who drove a red Ford Thunderbird convertible. Sometime he would give us money to buy lunch for the crew and toss us the keys to his car. We were like movie stars as we went to The Beacon, a nearby restaurant, to buy burgers. PW was my high school class sponsor and Doug, my classmate.

When you think about summers, the really good ones come to mind. This was mine. My best friend, Jimmy, and our pal, Martha, who we called Martie, were like the Three Musketeers. Martie was a year older and our birthdays were on the same day. If you remember railroad caps, the three of us wore them as a symbol of our connection. Whenever we were together, we wore those caps. It was a very innocent time and we loved Martie like the sister we never had.

In later years, I took her to dinner when I was in Washington DC on business. I had a car phone. There was one channel and the transmitter was in my trunk. My Oldsmobile 98 Luxury Sedan sported two aerials, one for the radio and one for my phone. As we drove around the Beltway, we called her "Bubba" who never did understand when Martie tried to explain that we were calling from my car.

Jay and I were fair guitar players and self-taught. Most songs were played in the key of E and had three chords and we sang in harmony. He was a year older, Byzantine Catholic, an altar boy, and we attended the same high school. When summer ended, we went our separate ways. I was an athlete and Jay was in the drama club.

I thought about my workmate and invited him to the next practice. He could sing, was a heartthrob and music was changing. The guitar was becoming a popular instrument and vocals were starting to explode in popularity. Remember Elvis Presley?

Jay came with an old Kay acoustic guitar. We had more practices and the band started to click. I played bass and sang the unusual songs because I had a big vocal range. The responsibility of singing lead fell on Jay who learned songs quickly. Bruce, who looked younger than his age, was a solid drummer. He idolized his neighbor, also a drummer. Wild Bill Davids & the Rockets were the pride of Struthers High. They were the most popular group in the area and following high school, Bill designed and sold for Rogers, a famous drum manufacturer. We started practicing at Bruce's home because the drums were always set up. After the war, many new homes were built as soldiers returned from war. The small house had two bedrooms, an unfinished attic, living room, kitchen, a basement and an unattached single car garage. It housed Earl's 1959 Chevy (remember big fins, huge trunk, four doors). His family included sisters, Carol and Michelle.

Danny, played the accordion and piano. He worried about everything. His greatest talent was an ability to keep us focused and prevent arguments. His mother was a saint; his father a drill sergeant.

Mouse was gifted. He played all saxophones, clarinet, flute and sang background vocals. His ability to hear a song then communicate the arrangement to the rest of the band was unbelievable. He could sight-read, was a perfectionist and had a brain wired for music. He became skilled in guitar, bass, engineering, song writing and composition. Mouse is imaginative and creative but also strange. He lives somewhere in outer space but is one of my best friends.

We learned songs by listening to records and figuring out words and chords. After a few attempts we'd do the tune better than the artist. We sang cover tunes, mostly vocals and no originals. We were so talented that we often learned songs while going to play.

Our vocalist and lead singer had a great voice for rock and roll. I believe he could have made it on his own but didn't have the fire in the belly and was lazy. Although he played guitar, it was strictly to accompany the vocals.

I became leader, front man and booking agent running every aspect of the band. Our income was split equally as we were all for one and one for all.

We were on our way or so I wished. I am a hard worker but knew I was lucky. God had a plan.

I enjoy people and for a few years we were a band of brothers who became the toast of the town. It was a great three-year run but ended on a sour note.

Sisters that *never* followed the band were: Cindy, related to Danny; Sue, related to Mouse, and Carol and Michelle, related to Bruce. I met Carol in 1961 but never paid attention to her.

She was in the National Honor Society, not interested in boys and the apple of her father's eye. Bruce had a paper route, but Carol delivered and collected money. She had a great personality for a serious girl and later bought a red Pontiac GTO.

Michelle, her younger sister, was a cute child who worked for Isaly's, a dairy store whose milk was popular. The ice cream and sherbet were delicious. Their signature products were chip-chopped ham and the Skyscraper. A special long scoop was designed to gather the ice cream so that it looked like a rocket when placed in a cone.

Their parents were Earl, a World War II veteran and crane operator in a steel mill, and Amelia "Millie," who had a beauty shop in their home.

Our dream was to play at the Elms Ballroom and Idora Park Ballroom, two well-known venues in

Northern Ohio. What should we call our group? I'm sure you've heard of the Platters, Crickets, Beach Boys. We decided to be The Del Rays.

Early in our band life, we traveled to Ridgeway, Kane, DuBois and St. Mary's in the mountains of Pennsylvania. We were booked into clubs by Louie, an agent. He handled our pay so we never knew what was charged and called him the One-Armed Bandit because he only had one arm. We never liked him but we worked. The Big Trout Inn, Kane Teen Club and Ridgeway Moose became regular stops.

Leo, owner of the Big Trout Inn, would walk around collecting money because bars couldn't have a cover charge at the door. He'd come by the stage and tell us to play more polkas. It was what his patrons wanted but we were not a polka band and tried to ignore him. The "Beer Barrel Polka" was a favorite.

Traveling the wilds of Pennsylvania was done in a 1953 Oldsmobile that belonged to our lead singer. We loaded the instruments, equipment and clothes in the trunk and back seat, then off we went.

During one trip we encountered a woman whose car was stuck in a ditch and stopped to help. She fell down a steep hill into a pool of water and I immediately ran to save her. I threw off my jacket and prepared to dive into the pool. Fortunately I didn't, it was shallow.

The area was dangerous. We'd drive down Boo Jack Hill, a forty-degree grade with escape exits so truckers who lost their brakes could stop before reaching the ninety-degree turn at the bottom.

We were returning home and I slid down an ice covered road into a car. The owner saw that I had damaged his tail light and the fender of our car. The fellow said not to worry, it happened more than once. We offered to pay him but he refused and joked about the incident. I was never forgiven by my bandmate for damaging his car.

Everywhere had live music and we started to get bookings. The Lester's owned a pharmacy and sponsored dances at St. Anthony's Hall. We had a good following but needed a break.

The Golden Pheasant was the first place where The Del Rays were advertised. It was on the West Side of Youngstown and most of our crowd was from the Southeast side of town. Hardly anyone was old enough to buy beer and our debut flopped.

We started to develop a stage presence but the lead singer and I were playing junk instruments, the band had no sound equipment and we were not union musicians which had some meaning.

To join Local 86, you paid an annual fee and three percent of your earnings based on a weekly report. Many places only hired union bands and a place that didn't could be placed on the black list. No union band could play there until fines were paid.

During the winter the Elms Ballroom was a popular place and booked only the top bands: Buddy Rich, Count Basie and Stan Kenton were regularly featured.

You could rent the Elms and on certain nights the "black and tan" brought in their stars: James Brown and the Famous Flames, Etta James, Aretha Franklin, BB King, Little Richard and many others on the "chitlin circuit."

Do you remember record hops? Every Friday the Elms had one after football games. Kids packed the place and admission was fifty cents. You got to watch "Boots" Bell, a popular disc jockey from radio station WHOT, spin records and a popular local band played three sets in between.

The popular bands that appeared there regularly were Del Sinchak and the Saints, Wild Bill Davids and the Rockets, Larry Ladd and the Lads and the Mike Roncone band. Del had a half-hour music program on WYTV in Youngstown.

Bruce and Danny always had friends who played in rival bands. There was competition in our world of music but it was good. It made you sharpen your musical and vocal skills and all the successful groups belonged to the American Federation of Musicians.

One Wednesday, Danny and Bruce were eating lunch at The Beacon, a popular burger joint and local hangout. Larry, a popular saxophone player arrived. He was coming from the hospital with a broken arm. His band was scheduled to play the Elms that Friday but he said he was going to cancel.

My two bandmates drove to the Elms and told Eddy, the manager, that he would be getting a cancellation call. He said Larry was booked but if he did, it would be difficult to get a good band on short notice. They pitched The Del Rays and Eddy said if it happened, he'd hire us. The call came and we got a huge break. However, we'd have to join the union and wear matching jackets which was then in style.

Our pal Billy and his band were not playing so we rented their tux jackets. Thursday we joined the union and my former guitar teacher who was the treasurer took our dues and swore us in.

The radio spots on WHOT were already produced and there was no way to change them. Everyone expected Larry and the Lads to appear, not The Del Rays. We were nervous when we took the stage dressed in faded red tux jackets with black lapels and marginal equipment. Thankfully, the Elms had a good sound system and a Steinway piano.

The kids arrived expecting a favorite band. Boots introduced us and we faced the crowd, an unknown group of five guys. The place grew silent and we opened with a Gary US Bond's song, "Quarter to Three," then sang every vocal in the Top 50.

I was the master of ceremonies and bantered with the audience. We were on our way and the people loved our show. We became regulars for the next three years. Nobody could sing, perform and entertain like The Del Rays. We were a happy band.

Success and many bookings followed. The union was happy, happy, happy as we paid plenty in work dues. My job as leader became easier. I traded my modified guitar with bass strings for a Fender Precision bass which became a collectable that I still play. I traded my Carvin and $125 for my new instrument with a hardshell case.

Every town had a summer dance hall. Ours was the Idora Amusement Park. They had a huge ballroom and each Friday it was dedicated to entertaining youth. We packed the place when we appeared.

Al, the manager, loved our band as did all the DJ's at WHOT. The station had a "HOT" day every summer and we were the local headliner. We shared the stage with celebrities like Del Shannon, The

Tokens, Link Wray and his Ray Men, Big D. Irwin, The Belmonts and many more. We were great at vocals and often upstaged the big acts.

The Silver Dollar Cafe & Lounge, a black and tan club, was located in Youngstown on East Federal Street. Henry, the owner loved us. The patrons were in awe because we were five white boys who did a great show and could sing blues and soul music. One night a customer threatened him and Norman, his bar tender/bouncer shot him. There usually wasn't trouble, but we appeared under an assumed name, Little Bruce and the Flames. The club was on the union "black list" but we liked playing there.

We backed some of the least known stars: Luther, the goddess of fire, and Willie St. John who had a terrible lisp but could sing great. We also backed Shake Dancers who are not strippers, and there were gays, transvestites, bisexuals and people who weren't sure of what they were.

One of our most exciting experiences was the night we sang a complete album of Isley Brothers tunes. We were on fire, in a groove and people started throwing paper money at us. We felt like stars!

Our clothes came from the Modern Clothing Company, a store that catered to the hip. A red cutaway jacket, black trousers, white shirt and dress boots became our uniform but vocals and showmanship were the key to our popularity.

Our lead singer was married with children and a full time job. He couldn't travel so we stayed within fifty miles of Youngstown and missed opportunities.

A mistake was to sign a recording contract with Tony who managed the Edsels. He recorded us on the cheap and nothing developed.

One of the best things for me to come out of The Del Rays was Carol, whose brother Bruce was our drummer. I was three years older and neither of us dated. A relationship began after we disbanded. Forty-six years ago we married and are still together.

By our third year, things started to go bad in the band. Personal problems, women, alcohol, laziness and friction (ego) were factors. Finally, it was over and the dream ended. Stardom and the big time never arrived. We had a short but great run.

Bruce went to DC (Arlington, Virginia), Danny joined another band and for a brief time, Mouse and I played music together with some other musicians. It didn't work so Mouse got a full time job in a steel mill. There was, and always would be, only one Del Rays made up of the five original members.

Work and School

Like many of you, I was paying my way through college. I was a second-year business student attending Youngstown University, hating every minute and confused. Parental pressure made me enroll but I wasn't serious.

The school was on semesters and I carried a full class schedule. I usually ended up dropping a class or failing one each semester. My grade point average was low. I got frustrated and left school without properly withdrawing and failed everything. I would learn the hard way to never burn a bridge.

I went to Washington DC with my drummer Bruce on a Sunday afternoon. I bunked with him until I got a job then moved into an apartment with a friend. I eventually joined the Chesapeake & Potomac Telephone Company of Virginia (part of the Bell System) as an installer-repairman. I worked hard to get there and now "the rest of the story."

I was fat so I shed 30 pounds in about thirty days to be considered for employment. I was confident I would be hired, however I failed the physical because I am color blind. I was floored. I thought weight was the only barrier to me being hired.

I asked the nurse who interpreted my physical whether there was any option. I was distraught. She said plant personnel had to deal with cables and color codes but offered me a cable matching test. She picked out ten pairs from a small cable and I had to match all to a larger cable or no job.

After struggling, I matched all but one pair. On the way out I asked if she would match the pair I couldn't find. She was unable to find it and laughingly exclaimed, "You passed!" That is how I became a color blind telephone man.

My roommate worked for the Navy Department as a scientist and was from Ohio. He'd constantly get in my face about education and say, "You don't want to be a working stiff all your life, do you?"

Ron graduated from Brown University, an Ivy League School, which he attended on an academic scholarship. While living together, he decided to take an advanced math course at George Washington University. After his first class he dropped his text book on a table in our small apartment and I never saw it move. If you're a single male you know dust.

We decided to drive home to Ohio for a few days. Four of us made the trip. One of our mutual friends, Tom, was in the Navy and stationed near Arlington. Periodically we'd give him a ride home. If Ron was a genius (which he was), Tom was a simpleton.

During a memorable trip back to DC, they got into discussion of Bernoulli's law of aerodynamics and argued for seven straight hours. Tom was putting

50

him on but Ron was serious. We had a good laugh as we listened. When we returned to our apartment He finally figured out that the joke was on him. I told him he needed to relax.

I returned from work one evening and found him thumbing through the pages of the math book. What's up? He was studying for his final the next night. Being a genius, he aced the course.

Ron looked like a mad scientist. He had a crewcut, was tall, gangly and had poor eyesight. His Coke bottle eye glasses helped. He couldn't walk and chew gum at the same time but could fly you to the moon. Finally, I decided to re-enter college.

When I returned to the university I was a changed person. Living in Arlington with my friend made a difference and I matured. I had to beg the Dean of the Business School to return and was permitted to go part time because of my low grade point average.

The school was now on quarters. The Dean closely followed me for two quarters before allowing me to go full time. I made all As while taking a light load. I also worked as a musician to pay for school.

It was the start of the Motown era and Mouse was with Kenny & the Casuals. Soul music was their forte. Kenny, the leader, played guitar. Ted was a talented Hammond B3 player and also played sax. Tom, his younger brother, was the drummer and a wild child. Mouse played sax and they brought me in to play bass. All of us could sing.

Ken heard I was difficult to get along with and so did one of the club owners where the band appeared. Crest Lanes, a bowling alley, also housed a popular night club and the band played there on a regular basis. When Johnny, the manager, heard I was going to join, he was concerned and said he wasn't going to book them if I became a player.

I met with him and his girlfriend, Sue, a bartender at the club. He got to the point. "I understand you are difficult." I assured him I would be a great addition to the band and suggested he contact a few people we both knew. We became good friends and I think Sue thought I was cute.

The Golden Stallion, a Warren, Ohio, night club and restaurant, was located in a tough part of town. They drew a young crowd of beer drinkers who demanded good music. The owner, Stephan, was a hard drinking man with a great personality. He liked the group because we packed the place.

His cook was an old woman who loved the band. Nearly every night we played, she would cook us a special meal after the club closed. Delicious garlic fried chicken, homemade fried onion rings and creamy coleslaw. We would feast. Stephan's best friend, a welder, was always bragging that he could weld anything. One night after many beers, we questioned his ability. He said he could weld our brains to our mouths if we liked. I was doing well at college.

I decided to throw a birthday party so I asked my girlfriend to have it at her home because it had a large, dry, partially finished basement. In the middle of activities, I surprised her with an engagement ring.

Her Aunt Ann and Uncle George lived near Pittsburgh and knew a jeweler they trusted. After her parents consented, the relatives took me to buy a ring. Carol was shocked and had no idea I planned to propose.

Six months later we chose a wedding date and I wanted a big party. I was a professional musician on the way to finishing college; the future looked bright.

If you were fortunate enough to have a mentor in your life, Dr. Dumitru Teodorescu was mine. He was the smartest and most difficult professor in the Youngstown Business School. He was a no-nonsense teacher from Romania who spoke broken English and was difficult to understand. He talked like my grandma so every word made sense to me.

His two earned doctorates were in economics, and library science. Doc T, as everyone called him, was brilliant. I was the only student who could properly

53

pronounce his name. He was short with long thinning hair combed forward over his bald spot, wore large glasses and was a vane person.

Having Teodorescu for every class he taught convinced the Dean that I was a changed man and serious. I finished three years in two, sometimes taking 20 hours, a heavy load in a university on quarters.

The old professor and I were cast from the same mold. I developed a tremendous respect for him and always sat in the front row. He would pace the room and lecture over his big glasses, long hair slipping off his bald spot. He'd look me straight in the eye, and say, "Isn't that right, Mr. Timciski?" He always called me, Timciski.

Bob, a friend of mine always sat in back of the class. One day, Doc T noticed him dozing off during a lecture. He stopped in the middle of the presentation and shouted, "Mr. Fiorelli, is this boring you?" The whole class broke up in laughter. Years later, Bob married my wife's cousin Linda.

My last name is Timcisko, but for Doc T, my name ended in "i." He had a huge intellect, and was a mentor. I received my Bachelor of Science in Business Administration degree and was in the first graduating class when Youngstown University became a state school.

I was always a planner. Running the business end of a band was helpful in organizing my wedding. We chose February because Carol would be twenty-one and I would be twenty-four. I compiled a list of things to do leading up to the wedding and started working. Our parents couldn't afford it so economy was everything. I'd have to pay most of the expenses.

I was marrying outside the Byzantine Catholic faith as Carol was Methodist, but I got permission to use my church hall for free. It was new, large and the senior ladies of the church catered weddings. I was a faithful altar boy and related to a founding member so the food was provided at cost. Once this was done the pressure was off and we only had small details to contend with.

The menu would be fried chicken, pasta, sauce and meatballs, salad, potatoes, sausage and peppers, bread and butter. I'd provide all the utensils and paper products. The women were the best cooks, and they all loved me, even though I was "sinning" by marrying outside the Catholic faith. I prayed it would work out and it did.

Next was the cake. We knew a person who only did wedding cakes so all we needed to know was the number of guests and what we wanted designed. Our families baked the pastry. I had many friends and contacts in all types of businesses.

Joe, who sold for a liquor company, supplied all the booze at cost. I could return what wasn't used. I knew a paper products wholesaler so all disposables were inexpensive. Jim, worked for a printing company and we got a deal on invitations. My friend Henry, an amateur photographer, did weddings and gave us a good price on albums. After the wedding he gave us all the photos he took as a gift.

Finally, what about the music? Being a professional union musician I had to hire a union band. There would be old, middle aged and young people at our affair. What to do? Money was an issue and the best bands were expensive. I had an idea worth a try.

I played electric bass, not upright like the symphony orchestra, and periodically filled in with a country club band, the Ernie Mitchell Quartet. Fred, the leader, liked the fact that I could play any type of music, wasn't loud and sang anything. The jobs I played with his band always included a meal, drinks, and paid a lot more than union scale.

I approached Fred and told him I was getting married and needed a band. The problem was money. He said the band would perform for three hours and only charge union scale. Our friends were treated to all types of great music and a big helping of polkas, waltzs and some rock and roll.

On Saturday, February 10, 1968, Carol Ann Dill became Mrs. Nicholas Timcisko at the Struthers, Memorial United Methodist Church, officiated by Reverend Miller. The reception was held at St. Michael's Byzantine Catholic Hall. It was a cold but sunny day with a light dusting of snow. Everything went off without a hitch and the day became one of our fondest memories.

We arrived at our small apartment and began life as a married couple. I had a cigar. Monday morning, I went to school so we didn't have a honeymoon.

Our new residence was owned by Mrs. Kessler, a widow and wealthy member of Carol's church. Her huge home was split into three apartments. She lived on the first floor and only rented to newly married couples. She interviewed us in July and held the apartment until our wedding without any charge.

Judy and Rich lived on the second floor and we were next door. It was wonderful to have friends nearby and often visited. Rich's cousin moved to the third floor apartment with his wife and we were one happy commune.

Mrs. Kessler allowed us to paint, decorate and bring our furniture. A friend, Paul, installed carpeting in the living room. Today it covers part of my finished basement and is as a remembrance of early days.

Graduation from college was in sight and interviews were plentiful: Libby Owens Ford, a glass company, Sears, the retailer, Standard Oil of Ohio, a petroleum giant who owned the "Pro Brush" Division, Meryl Lynch, a brokerage firm, IBM, a computer giant and Xerox, the premier copier company. I was older than my classmates, a professional musician and married. It was great being courted and recruited by many companies.

I chose Xerox because they had a glamorous name, was a leader in their industry and market driven. The deciding factor was they offered to employ me before graduation. I'd finish school getting paid.

Most love to talk about their family and I'm no different. Maybe you can relate since mine is typical.

Lori Diane, my oldest daughter, was born twelve months after our marriage in Youngstown. On the morning of January 2, 1969, I kissed Carol goodbye and drove to a meeting in Erie, Pennsylvania, sixty miles away. Sal, manager of the Youngstown office, also ran the sales office in Erie. Carol, late in her pregnancy, planned to go shopping with her mom.

Later in the day I called home and got no answer. Remember, this is before cell phones. I finally learned that she was at the hospital in labor. It was a snowy, cold, windy, miserable gray day. I was panicked. There I was stuck in Erie.

Tom, one of the senior sales representatives from Youngstown, was a pilot. We discussed chartering a plane but it was a dangerous day to fly so it wasn't an option. I stayed for the meeting and came home to a baby girl.

Today, Lori and spouse Daryle have a specialty advertising and printing business, Keith Marketing Group in Indianapolis, Indiana. They both graduated from Kent State and the business is a Female Business Enterprise (FBE). Lori is active in the business but her primary focus is being a mother to Kayla, Tyler and Jennifer.

Kayla recently graduated from Westfield High school and attends college. Tyler is a junior and the family moved to Carmel because he is a great baseball player and they have a better sports program. The hope is that this will result in a scholarship. Ty trains at a private facility, Round Trippers, a place with wonderful coaching and an indoor baseball field.

Jennifer, the youngest, is athletic and plays volleyball and softball. She will start high school in a few years. She has an outgoing personality, my sense of humor and is stubborn like her father.

My son, Scott, quit college and lived in Atlanta, Georgia, for ten years. He returned home without any sense of direction and through a friend, I got him a job parking cars at Hillcrest Hospital. He was hired by the hospital to answer the phone. Like his dad, he has a great personality and is smart like his mother. He married and lives ten miles away.

They had a child, Sophia and opportunity struck. The Cleveland Clinic owns Hillcrest and offered him a chance to become a CAT Scan Technician. He went to school full time on their nickel, worked part time, received his certification and the Clinic hired him. A second child, Maria, arrived as he was finishing school. His marriage came apart and he divorced. Scott now lives with us and has the girls every other week. Sophia is high strung and strong willed. She's beautiful, artistic and studies Kuc Sol Do (a martial art). Scott is a great father and works with her.

Today, a fidgety child full of energy and a short attention span has a disability. Medication and counseling is the answer to what can be corrected by restoring gym class. Children have no way to burn their energy and most don't listen. (Does this bring back memories?).

Maria, a humorous five-year-old, is always thinking, learns fast and deeply loves us. She, like many children developed skills while watching TV and videos. She has a guitar, strums it properly, sings with good pitch and is my last hope that music will

60

continue as a tradition. None of my other grandkids are interested in music other than the radio.

I had my antique 1957 Fender duo sonic guitar restored and asked if she liked the instrument. She said yes so if she learns the guitar, I told her it will be hers. I plan to send her to my friend Steve for lessons. I'm having her evaluated by the Cleveland Institute of Music and the Cleveland Music Settlement to decide the next step.

She is petite and cute as a button. When I ask for a kiss, she'll tell me the kiss truck comes tomorrow. However, there are plenty of kisses for granny and her daddy who she loves.

Tiffany, our youngest is twice divorced and has three children: Julia, Nicholas and Matthew. Life is not easy. She has psoriasis and battles depression but works as an escrow clerk for a major real estate company. They were living with us when Scott arrived with his two girls.

Having nine people in a five bedroom home with only two and a half baths is challenging. There was always a lot going on and we are senior citizens. You do what you have to do. I always told my children that as long as Carol and I were alive they would have a home. They took me up on it. We share a lot of love in tight quarters. This was soon to change.

Today I'm teaching my fourteen-year-old grandson, Nicholas, which end of a nail you pound in a wall. I send him for a channel lock and he brings a vice grip. Youngsters are totally ignorant about tools or how to fix anything. They know computers, how to play video games and texting on their cell phones. I ask them not to use these devices when they visit.

Julia, sixteen, should super glue the phone to her arm. She is constantly texting or calling. I got her a job at our local Panera Bread but she quit. She hopes to attend college and is considering nursing. She is a beautiful girl and a smart young woman.

Matthew, her youngest, is slow. He has a tutor at school and his favorite word is "can't." He's a sweet boy with a high pitched voice that won't change soon enough. He loves his grandmother's cooking and is at our home all the time. I tease him about inventing something to become rich. He needs an assistant to be at his call. He said when he did invent a moneymaker, he would get granny a man servant. He has a kind heart.

Tiffany's family recently moved into a condo across the street from my home. It was the answer to alleviating congestion. We are now down to five people and have enough bedrooms and baths.

Xerox

I was hired by Xerox Corporation before I graduated from Youngstown State University in August, 1968. My first sales territory included parts of Youngstown and the New Castle-Elwood City area in Pennsylvania. I sold to all markets which included everything from large corporations to accountants and law firms.

Xerox had a sales training center in Ft. Lauderdale nicknamed "Xerox U" in the Sheraton Hotel where I went for two weeks of training. It is a fun town during spring break and loaded with women.

New Xerox sales trainees stayed in the Windholm Hotel, located across from the Sheraton. The company leased the complex and two people shared a typical hotel room.

My roommate, Barney, was captain of the University of Texas Longhorns and was built like a fire hydrant. He taught me about always playing to win and knew all about big oil.

Irving Pincus ran the school, and Dick Blattner, was second in command. Both Jewish New Yorkers were smart. I remember the welcome to Xerox meeting and speech when Irv held up a wad of dollars and explained that we were here to make money for the company and ourselves. It wasn't totally about greed but you get it. Would you go to work for no pay?

Each day class started at nine. Sales Training was about listening, prospecting, probing and closing the sale. Can you see the picture? Our favorite trial close was the word, "Oh," followed by silence.

It was intense but fun. I was happy because I was getting paid to attend. It was quite a change from life at college. Xerox's "Professional Selling Skills" was one of the best sales courses I've ever taken.

The best course I ever took was the "Effective Listening Course" designed to teach you how to hear. Before starting you completed a write-up from memory of a recorded conversation. I filled a paragraph. You took the course which included tapes and workbook. It seemed a waste of time. It was mandatory and every sales person had to complete it before attending the sales school. You listened to a conversation, stopped the tape and wrote an answer in the work book. Finally after two hours you were done and asked to listen to a different conversation. I filled over a page with comments on what I heard and realized the course was amazing. It should be mandatory for everyone.

My life was turned upside down when my mother had a brain aneurysm and surgery. It left her paralyzed, unable to complete a sentence and depressed. It took ten years to get her to open the drapes in her living room and she spent her life in a chair, smoking and sad. She became a vegetable. My step-father and I bought a duplex to make things easier for mom. This provided a place for us to live.

She wouldn't leave home except to go to the doctors and never visited any other home where we lived: Poland, Ohio (five miles), Rochester New York, Newport News, Virginia, or Chagrin Falls, Ohio. It was heartbreaking.

When I sold in Youngstown, one of my customers was Carmen Policy, a young attorney in the Legal Arts Center. He became an executive with the Cleveland Browns and later the San Francisco 49ers.

The California team was owned by Youngstown shopping mall developer, Ed DeBartolo Sr. His son became president of the team and he and Carmen were best friends. Junior lost control when he became involved in a gambling scandal. Greed is not good.

Jerry, a fellow salesman, had a big personality and full figure. He developed a health issue and lost forty pounds. When I asked how he did it, he said Uncle Herman, a shoe salesman from Pennsylvania. He is a hypnotist and works closely with Sharon Hospital.

He conducted weight loss sessions in his living room for five to eight people on certain evenings. I was interested because I was fat all my life and now obese. His sessions were booked but someone cancelled and I filled a spot. We were comfortably seated in his living room but it seemed too good to be true. Here are seven people listening to a shoe salesman telling us what hypnosis wasn't. You couldn't be told to do anything against your will and would be awake. If you started to doze off he'd wake you; then came his "rap."

There was a flow of information saying what you would not desire and I caught myself dozing and so did Herman. When he ended, I was skeptical and thought nothing had changed. He said some will stop on the way home and have some kind of sweet. You really won't want it but upon eating it the spell would be gone along with ten dollars and two hours.

Some of you will reject fattening food for a time then weaken and eat something sweet and be back on the bad track. As long as you didn't do the wrong thing, it would work. I told Herman I didn't feel any different but he said, "Trust me" this works.

The next day, I attended my nephew's birthday party and sat in front of the cake. The fumes were overwhelming but I was able to resist temptation. I remained in this mode for nearly a year and lost over fifty pounds. Then I weakened and ate one sweet and found myself back on the fat track. I gained back all my old weight and more.

A few months after the meeting, I met Herman for lunch because I was interested in memory development but still skeptical. He said it was easy to hypnotize yourself and demonstrated. Are you strong? "Yes," I said. He placed his hand on the counter, concentrated for a minute and asked me to lift it. I could not do it. This feat made a believer out of me. Herman is now dead but his daughter continues to do hypnosis. It is real, amazing and it works.

I did well as a sales representative and was promoted to a staff position at Xerox's headquarters in Rochester, New York. I joined a small group that analyzed and reported on competition. We served the key executives and field sales force. I was a spy.

If you've ever watched a James Bond movie, you've heard a suave sophisticated voice say, "My name is Bond, James Bond." Then Agent 007, who is ruggedly handsome and smooth, is equipped with all kinds of gadgets and drinks martinis. He is a ladies man and always in action. Only in the movies!

My job was to read a mountain of reports and write a short document, the monthly "Competitive Activity Report." Our mission was to conduct industrial espionage. My partner, John, and I visited trade shows and attended annual meetings to gather info.

During one trade show, the price list of our major competitors fell into my briefcase. I was also a dumpster diver before the era of the shredder. It's amazing what companies throw in the trash. I evaluated competitive products and created detailed data sheets to help sales.

My partner and I were attending a show in Washington DC and arrived a day early. We had a few too many drinks that evening and were one of the first to enter the convention center the next morning.

A man was taking pictures and our mugs would soon appear in "Reprographics," a monthly trade magazine. The beginning of an article describing the show featured a photo of us looking around. I was sporting a hangover and John was running slow.

Our boss, Len, was one of the first to see the magazine and wasn't happy about us appearing in print. Many of our field contacts sent notes asking how two spies received such coverage. We got razzed and this wasn't stardom.

Jack, one of our associates was promoted to sales manager and relocated to Virginia Beach. I was happy for him. Staff work was fine but I missed being in the field. I was under pressure when my boss was placed under a new manager.

Harvey was a ruthless man brought in to reorganize the staff operation. He was tough to work for; always making promises to the executives which were demanding. We were understaffed but Harvey didn't care. He was out to make a name for himself.

During our first meeting he gave me an article entitled "The Theory of Completed Staff Work." When we were given assignments, it was our responsibility to complete them and he would take the credit. We existed to make him look good.

A commitment was made to the president that would require work in a ridiculously short time. I was given the assignment and spent fifteen hours a day to make the deadline. The subordinates all called him "Harvey the hatch(et)." He started cleaning house. I was probably saved from getting axed because I got tasks done and was a friend of his boss Dave, a vice president. He was my regional manager when I was in field sales. We were friends and smoked cigars. I had some protection but others weren't so lucky.

Rochester is a city where the sun hardly shines. Pressure from Harvey and me slipping into a state of depression started to take its toll. I had enough and wanted out. It was either back to field sales or I would leave the company.

Although I was a staff analyst, I was in the loop and six levels away from the president who was being replaced. Our senior VP was being considered but corporate politics was alive and he left Xerox to become president of LTV. I followed his career. Every year the company lost money and he received a bonus. Life is not fair.

Harvey praised me because I made him look good but the pressure was too much and I requested a transfer. My staff partner, John, was instrumental in keeping me from a nervous breakdown. He suggested I contact our friend Jack in the Norfolk Branch about a job. Jack agreed to hire me but I'd have to pay my way to Virginia. It was a way out of Rochester which I grew to hate. I took a vacation.

I visited my mentor, Dr. Teodorescu, who was now Chairman of the Business School at YSU. I found his office where he was reading some papers deep in thought and gently tapped on the door. He looked over his glasses and I said, "Dr. Teodorescu, you probably don't remember me." With eyes like laser beams he said, "Mr. Timcisko, Dr. Teodorescu never forgets anything." We had a long discussion.

I moved to Virginia and Carol was left to sell the house. It was the change I needed. The Tidewater area is beautiful, the sun always shined and I got away from Harvey. Although Jack was my boss, I lived with him and his family until I rented a room.

Jack's sales area included: the Army at Fort Monroe, home of the Continental Army Command (CONARC), Fort Eustis (Transportation School),

Tactical Air Command (TAC) and NASA located at Langley Air Field.

I was brought in to save the Air Force which had become vulnerable to competition but things did not look promising. Jack believed I could stabilize the situation. It was tricky. I managed to solidify the two Army accounts and NASA.

The Air Force put their total reprographic needs out for a competitive bid and every Xerox product was removed. However, I set the stage and Xerox recaptured the account a year later.

I was an asset to the Army and during my tenure, I worked closely with the directors of many departments. I received a special pass which permitted me to park anywhere on the post at Fort Monroe where parking is a major problem.

My three main contacts at CONARC were John, a typical bureaucrat, his subordinate Everett, whose goal was to be promoted, and Mike, a Chief Warrant Officer whose was located in another building. Mike was my most important contact. I developed a solid relationship and they saw I was a problem solver.

I also cultivated a relationship with the Director of Purchasing. Things were dynamic in the Army and after responding to a couple of issues that demanded my time and attention, I was given an open purchase order even though I was a salesman.

I'd work with my military contacts to recommend the Xerox product they needed and place the order. Then I'd report to Purchasing who filled in the blanks. It was efficient, effective and good for all. I was a trusted asset and considered one of the team. I did right for the Army even though I benefitted as well.

Copy paper was manufactured for Xerox by Hammermill in Erie, Pennsylvania. I once toured their facility and knew the process and the quality Xerox demanded. Our paper was sold at a premium price and worked best in our machines.

Mike was responsible for buying all paper and toner, the black thermoplastic powder used in the Xerographic process. We had a sale on paper and if you bought a freight carload you got a great price. It was a huge amount of paper and was shipped by rail on wooden pallets in a boxcar.

Fort Monroe had a railroad siding, huge warehouse and could easily handle the shipment. I convinced Mike that it would be a good investment. The post was using a large amount of copy paper so he agreed to the buy and I wrote the order.

Near the end of the fiscal year, there was money in his budget and I suggested another carload if there was space. Mike agreed and I ordered again. When it arrived he asked if I had ever seen two freight cars of paper. I had not, so we drove to a warehouse and when we walked into the secure location my mouth dropped.

There were three special tow motors stacking the pallets of paper on steel shelving that went from the floor to the ceiling. It was a sight to behold. Mike was happy because I got early billing and depleted his budget. I was happy because I made a large commission.

IBM entered the copy business while I handled Fort Monroe and assigned their top man to the account, a young fellow named Jim. He was a hot shot who looked like a movie star. The typewriter sales representative, Jules, who I considered a friend, was losing the account to "Jimmy." My Xerox friends in the Navy were happy because he was being moved to the Army account. They believed he was going to clean my clock.

Jules was introducing his replacement to the brass and we crossed paths. He introduced me to Jimmy, who was young and cocky. He fit the IBM mold; tailored suit, button-down white shirt, tall, good looking and over confident. He dismissed me as if to say, you are history.

To be truthful I was concerned because he had given fits to the Xerox sales team handling the Navy. He was good. Soon, he was contacting all the right people but not following the rules. I also was independent but knew how to play within the system. I started to see him everywhere on the post.

One day while meeting with the control group of Everett and John, I asked if there was a new policy. I knew Mr. IBM wasn't following protocol and mentioned that he was meeting with people without reporting to them. He was going to the top which is the IBM way. I always briefed them on my activities and they were upset with the information. The two civilians ran the show. Soon after this, the Xerox Navy team in Norfolk said rumor had it that Jimmy was returning to the Navy and my old friend Jules was going back to the Army.

Because of his cockiness and not following the rules (and a little bird who informed the right people), he was banned from the post by my contacts. I was happy because I was now totally in the driver's seat. What I didn't know is that my boss was being promoted and a new manager was taking over the Norfolk operation.

I was at the top of my sales game and things were great. My boss became a Branch Sales Manager in a different city, business was excellent and I knew I was making things happen.

74

This was a point where God was absent in my life and I didn't attend church. Every Sunday, Carol and the children went to the Warfield Memorial United Methodist Church in the Denbigh area of Newport News and I played tennis.

Pastor Bill was a big, jovial man who I liked. I attended Fish Fry at the church on Fridays in the summer. He always invited me to church but never pressured me to go and I didn't because I was busy.

One day the he called and asked if I could usher for a month, to which I adamantly said, "I'm not a member of your church." He said, "I don't care. We need help because of vacations. Will you help?"

I was shocked and uncomfortable but didn't have anything planned for the month. So I showed up at church four Sundays in a row, dressed in a suit and tie. After the stint, I returned to my summer ritual of tennis on Sunday mornings.

The air waves started to fill with the news that Billy Graham, the great evangelist, was coming to the Norfolk/Newport News area to have a "Crusade." I couldn't stand Billy Graham but recognized a good salesman and knew he was one of the best. His team announced that he would speak in Newport News on November 2, 3, 4 at the Hampton Roads Coliseum. I was intrigued. I knew he had a great pitch and all successful salespeople are able to close the deal. I decided to attend the first meeting to watch his technique. I was lost and full of myself at this time in my life.

I showed up the first night and listened. The guy was good. I knew commitment when I heard and saw it. The man was committed to the message of Jesus Christ. At this time in my spiritual life I was an agnostic and searching. I didn't tell Carol and she suspected nothing because I went to late business meetings. I was impressed with Graham. He was impeccable in dress and speech and knew what he was talking about. He claimed the Bible was "The Word of God" and often referred to it when he spoke.

I returned to hear him for the two additional nights he spoke in Newport News. On the last evening, I bought the soft cover version of his autobiography and went to my seat. I didn't think I was paying attention to the message but just observing.

After every meeting Billy Graham concludes with an invitation to turn your life over to Christ. For years, I believed the term "born again" was a media creation; something that advertising wizards had invented. I realized it meant becoming a new person headed in a new direction and following a plan God has for you.

My rationale became, what if Billy Graham is right? It sounded like I needed to be reborn to a new life since my old one wasn't great. I had nothing to lose and everything to gain. When he made the call I headed to the platform ready to take a major step in my life. Graham spoke his heart, certain of the message and confident in Jesus Christ.

About 200 of us prayed this prayer with Billy. These are my words: Lord, I am a sinner. Forgive me, I am not deserving of your mercy. Thank you for sending Your Son, Jesus, to die for me that I might be saved from damnation and separation from you. I accept Jesus Christ as my Savior and repent of my sin. Come into my heart, control my life and help me.

I met with a counselor who had me sign a card with the date of my new birth. The card was for me and I carry it in my Bible. He also gave me a package of material which included a Gospel of John and some other relevant material.

I was leaving the auditorium with my package and the book about Billy Graham and met Mr. Graham. We spoke and he wrote "God bless you," autographed it and scribbled something after his name (Phil 1:6).

What a three-day experience it had been! I began to wonder what I had done. One immediate change I implemented was to start attending church with my family. It was the beginning of a walk that continues to this day.

Tim, my new sales manager was paranoid and claimed to be a former Navy Seal. No matter what I said or did, he believed I was after his job which I was not. I was comfortable with the Army, NASA and Air Force. I was sure that TAC at Langley Field would come back to Xerox and I wanted to be around when it happened. It would be a big payday.

He started to pressure me, wanting more business out of the Army and demanded I press my key contact at NASA. I explained we had over ninety percent penetration of the Army and more could result in disaster. If the Department of Defense sent an audit team, it could result in a bid program. This is what happened at the Air Force, which resulted in a total loss for Xerox.

Phil, the new Branch Manager, was meek. He relied on his sales managers and wouldn't listen to any field representative like me. I was moved out of my assignment when I refused to pressure my NASA contact. To me it would have been the kiss of death. I was demoted and replaced by a good friend.

I was in a low place and going back to a territory as a sales representative bruised my ego. I still had to deal with my paranoid boss. My new branch manager didn't know me and I was intimidated.

And now I wouldn't participate in the financial success when the Air Force came back to Xerox.

In mid-1975, Carol's mom died suddenly and it took a toll on me. Millie and I didn't always agree but she never meddled in our affairs and I grew to love her. She was wonderful to our three young children and visited our home wherever we lived. I was always happy to have her.

To close this chapter, please meet a colleague who I met when I started with Xerox and who became one of my best friends. Harold Davis, who is African-American, was an All-American in basketball and football at Westminster College in New Wilmington, Pennsylvania. HD was inducted into the college Hall of Fame in South Bend, Indiana in 2004. My father-in-law, a sports fan and umpire, said Harold was the best high school quarterback he ever watched play.

I attended his induction ceremony which was an interesting three-day event. I met such greats as: Joe Theisman, a quarterback with the Washington Redskins, and Barry Sanders a great running back, to name a few.

Theisman, a great guy, mingled with people, signed autographs (especially for kids) and is a humorous speaker. Sanders was a jerk. You had to purchase his book or he would not give you the time of day. It was a memorable event.

Many of Harold's former teammates at Westminster were there to support him. It was quite an experience. I loved Harold and Shirley Davis. On December 9, 2007, Harold lost a long time battle with cancer. He helped me and many others along the way in life and has a beautiful family. His legacy of service is a testimony to a successful life. His presence will always be felt and he is greatly missed.

Ohio

If you've ever had a catastrophe change the direction of your life, this chapter will bring back memories. The best laid plans can change.

Carol worried about her father, following my mother-in-law's death, because they were extremely close. We decided it was time to go back to Ohio. I submitted a formal request to transfer but never heard anything. During a visit to Youngstown and after eight great and interesting years with Xerox, I took a job with Pitney Bowes, the world leader in postage meters. They were in the process of introducing a copier and believed I would be an asset. We prepared to move. I was uncomfortable selling their products and as a company they were nothing like Xerox.

The housing market was slow when we put our home in Newport News up for sale. I was in Ohio for a few months before things were finalized.

I learned that Carol's dentist was selling his home in Poland, Ohio, and purchased it. I didn't use a realtor on either end so the saving paid for our move. Our friends, Al and Vivian, who were much older, came from Ohio to Virginia and helped. Carol babysat for their five children when she was young.

I watched enough professional movers over the years so I rented a truck and knew to pack tight. I held the bottom of the roll-down door and slammed it closed, as I shoved in the last item. We were on our way to a new adventure.

Shortly after we arrived, my father-in-law met a woman in a bar, married and walked out of our lives. We rarely had anything to do with him after that and it seemed like our move was a mistake.

Pete, the Xerox branch manager in Akron which included Youngstown, was a friend. He heard I was back in town and had his sales manager arrange a meeting. He asked why I didn't contact him. My transfer request never crossed his desk. I was rehired and my time bridged. It was like I never left.

Xerox had changed. There were more salespeople, my territory was small and the compensation plan was totally different. After a few years of struggle, I decided to look for a new job.

On July, 1978, I joined the marketing department of the Ohio Bell Telephone Company (OBT) in Youngstown. In the early 1960s, I worked for the plant department of the C&P Telephone Company in Arlington, Virginia.

Both companies were part of the Bell System. I knew the culture of a utility company, but there was a movement starting and "market driven" were the new buzz words. They seemed headed in the right direction for me.

I was confident that my phone company experience, coupled with ten years at Xerox, had positioned me for an explosive career. Ohio Bell wanted to become sales oriented and Xerox provided me with a solid base. I was ambitious and it seemed like the right fit at the time. My sales group reported to Akron and shortly after I started, the company asked me to relocate to Cleveland. I viewed this as a good opportunity since Youngstown was becoming a ghost town.

They offered me a package that included paying for the move and all the costs associated with selling my home and buying a home in Cleveland. I would get a pay raise and lodged in a downtown Cleveland hotel until everything was settled. It was a great incentive package and I was happy. I reported to the marketing department on Bolivar Street for my assignment and began looking for a home.

While house shopping, Carol and I stumbled upon a new development near Chagrin Falls, a quaint version of a small New England town located in Cuyahoga County. The downtown Chagrin Triangle is surrounded by restaurants, shops and historical buildings. A river with a beautiful falls runs through middle of town.

Bainbridge Township is next to Chagrin Falls in rural Geauga County and the development was called Bainbrook. I never considered building a

83

home but we liked one model. There were thirty existing homes, a clubhouse, two tennis courts and a pool. Because it was designated a Planned Unit Development all the lots were a half acre instead of the usual five-acre minimum.

I wanted to build on the lot across from the clubhouse because I could grill, take a dip in the pool and I played tennis. We had three young children and the street dead ended. The home we liked could be built on the property and "Living Homes" could get us special financing, based on my salary.

For five years we only needed to pay the interest. By then my projected income would handle the monthly payment. It was a stretch and we discussed the idea on the way back home.

With a down payment of one thousand dollars we could start the process of building a hundred thousand dollar home. That day we got a check for exactly a thousand dollars and viewed it as a positive sign. We signed to build and our home was scheduled to be completed by January 1979.

It would be a two-story colonial with five bedrooms, two-and-a-half baths, living room, dining room, family room, kitchen, laundry room and attached two-car garage and the large basement would be partially finished. We were now owners (with the bank) of our dream home. There were a few surprises along the way. We learned that allowances didn't get you much so upgrades and extras added to the cost. Landscaping was not included, also a big expense.

The extension of the State Route 422 to Cleveland was scheduled to be completed. It would make the drive to my office downtown about thirty minutes. Kenston was an excellent school system for our children, which was important.

Early into the building program I started to have mixed feelings. There were nickel and dime issues and I was getting cold feet but Carol insisted we press on. I was in the early stage of a mental break down.

I never talked about personal issues because I was afraid of being labeled insane. Carol's aunt spent years in and out of the Woodside Receiving Hospital, our local asylum, and suffered from depression. She was a regular visitor who went from pill to pill and doctor to doctor. It wasn't my idea of a happy life.

We made the move and in the spring I put in the lawn. Raking rocks and digging boulders out of the clay soil was backbreaking. I seeded, fertilized and watered, watered, watered. Little "grassers" as I call them begin to sprout. Thirty-six years later I have a beautiful lawn. It's not perfect but I did it.

What to do about shrubs? We spoke to a local man who owned Leuty's Nursery. Phil graduated from Ohio State in forestry and said most homes in our development were being oversold on trees and shrubs. In a few years people were going to face a mess.

He made a recommendation that fit our budget and jokingly asked if I knew how to use a shovel. Our selection was delivered and placed where they should go. I dug the holes and planted the shrubs.

During a summer picnic sponsored by Campus Life, a Christian young adult ministry, I volunteered to cook burgers. My helper Lenny, owned an upscale beauty salon and Carol needed a hairdresser.

His shop was expensive and we were struggling, financially. Lenny insisted that I have her visit and said, "I'll cut her hair for free." The place was large and the patrons rich. After he cut her hair he told her "Thank you, I'll see you again." He did it at no charge for a few years.

I started to have doubts about my job. Ohio Bell didn't seem receptive to a new type of selling. Most of the people in Marketing came from the ranks and were now Management. The Plant Department and Marketing Department didn't communicate.

I was dead-ended and assigned a business sector that made no sense to me, the burglar alarm market. What do you sell to the burglar alarm market? My main product was circuitry. This is the wiring that connected your home or business to a central office. There was always a problem with on-time delivery. I became involved with the industry and the relationship with Ohio Bell was cordial at best.

I joined the state alarm association and hoped to improve relations. My years with Xerox taught me how to move fast and be effective. Neither quality was appreciated at Bell, a public utility that moved at the speed of molasses in January (slow).

My first boss in Akron was a good person but a typical utility company manager. When I arrived in Cleveland my new boss was incompetent.

I was too eager and assertive, and started making people nervous. Marketing at Ohio Bell was a 9-to-5 job. I had never worked that way before and you were not supposed to interact with plant or field personnel. We were Management and thus started my demise.

The final blow came when the new vice president of AT&T Marketing, who was recruited from IBM, came to Cleveland for a meeting. He was standing before the Marketing Department but didn't look IBM. He was short, wore an open collar shirt, Gucci loafers and a sport coat. When he spoke, his lips dripped with honey as the sweet words of nothing flowed from his mouth. He left such an impact that I don't remember his name. He told us he was from the great IBM and was all being and all knowing.

I'd seen a similar scenario at Xerox when IBM entered the copier business. They pirated an executive from "Big Blue" and made him a senior VP. His whole pitch was, "I can't tell you things because of a confidentiality agreement but trust me I know what I'm talking about."

These men were paid big money to spread manure. In my covert staff role I was well aware of what was happening in the communications world. He didn't last and neither did the little hitter from AT&T.

Did you ever do something really dumb when you worked? I quit and went to nothing. This move contributed to our worsening financial problems. When you have a mortgage, property taxes, water bill, electric, trash pickup, development fees and assessments, it is not good to be unemployed.

Perhaps you have never done anything like this but it was a stupid thing for a man with three children and stay-at-home spouse to do. I regret it to this day.

I was always insecure and had many bouts with depression over the years. I came close to a nervous breakdown in Rochester but I believed that mental illness was a thing to be ashamed of like divorce. It was something my generation didn't address. I even started to question my Christianity.

Years later, by the grace of God, I got help. I was diagnosed as bi-polar and placed on medication. It takes courage to face your demons and persistence to overcome them. Sometime you have neither. Too much had been building up in me and I was headed for destruction. I had been sick for a long time.

I spent most of my life in Northeast Ohio. For years, Cleveland was the big city center of our world. It's a great town that suffered from a lot of negative observations. She was called "the mistake on the lake" and our sports world lived with much sorrow.

Janet Cho cited some of our sadder moments in the July 13, 2014, edition of *The Plain Dealer* newspaper. "…the Drive, The Fumble, The Move, The Shot, and our latest The Decision." Everyone is excited about the return of basketball great LeBron James to the Cleveland Cavaliers in the NBA.

James, a tremendously talented basketball star from Akron, Ohio, who initially signed with the Cavaliers in 2002, left for the Miami Heat in 2009. During his time there, the Heat won two championships.

When he was young and the toast of the town, LeBron left Cleveland in a way that soured many.

We love our sports teams and people are loyal fans. However, we have been denied a winner for years.

The Cleveland Browns departed for Baltimore in 1995 when Art Modell moved the team. It devastated the town. When they returned as a new team in 2002, so did hope.

The Indians baseball team has always struggled and Larry Dolan, the current owner, tried to bring home a winner but without great success. His son, Paul, is very involved and there is hope.

The Cleveland Cavaliers basketball team was purchased in 2005 by Dan Gilbert a wealthy businessman. Cleveland sports fans held their breath and hoped a high school star, LeBron James, could lead them to victory. When he departed for South Beach in 2010 things didn't look bright and our team fell on hard times.

Today, I am happy to say that we are excited by the return home of our local son. LeBron is in his prime and at the top of his game. I confess, I am not a big sports fan but my wife, Carol is a committed and engaging fan. I am happy for her and all the loyal people of northeast Ohio. The town is energized.

Cleveland has been chosen to host the 2016 Republican convention. Perhaps more importantly, LeBron returned. Within 48 hours of the announcement, season tickets for the Cavaliers sold out. I've never seen anything like it.

Kids are usually big sports fans and my grandson, Tyler, who lives in Carmel, Indiana is a huge Indians, Browns and Cavaliers fan. Naturally, he has to take a lot of abuse. I sent him a copy of *The Plain Dealer* that heralded LeBron's return and here is the rest of the story.

A few years ago when Tyler's father, Daryl, took him to a Cavaliers-Pacers game in Indiana, they sat in seats near the basket. During the game LeBron, on a power drive, ended up in Tyler's lap.

After the game, James returned and gave my grandson his personalized wristband. He has it prominently displayed in his bedroom, near the Indians and Browns memorabilia that adorns his walls.

Not to worry, Ty, there is hope that you and millions of Cleveland fans will one day celebrate a championship. Today, there is a lot of hope.

The Cigar Shop

The famous Broadway play and movie, "Fiddler on the Roof," takes place in the small, remote village of Anatekvah, Russia. The villagers are characters. There is Tevyeh (milkman), Golde (nagging wife), Rabbi (religious man), Lazar Wolfe (butcher), Yente (matchmaker), Motel (tailor) and Constable (police chief), to name a few.

Somewhere along life's way, did you ever find a place where everybody knows your name? It usually is a good thing. Think about your contacts with people over time as you take a journey with me.

I started smoking cigars in 1961. I was 17 years old and had a popular rock and roll band, the Del Rays. Paula, a cute, petite girl, would bring me a bundle of cigars whenever she came to hear us play.

My favorite was the Cuesta Rey #95 green, a big size cigar. I bought them at Pans, a cigar shop on West Federal Street in Youngstown, near the Warner Theatre, now the DeYor Center.

The owner said he had an exclusive on them. You've heard that kind of claim, right? When I traveled I'd find a shop and look for that cigar. I never found it. Pan shipped a few boxes to me on a regular basis wherever I lived: Youngstown, Ohio, Rochester, NY, Newport News, Virginia, and Poland, Ohio. By the time I moved to Cleveland, 36 years ago, Pan was long gone to eternity and the shop closed.

There were 20 cigars in a plain wooden box with a simple clasp to keep it closed. I have some old boxes that I use for storage. Recently I read the label on the bottom of the box. The cigars were meant to sell for at least twenty cents. Are you laughing? That is an unheard of price for a cigar today.

We've all decided to stop something, either for a break or for good and I stopped smoking cigars. A few years went by.

My friend Jim, who was the best man in our wedding, returned from a vacation when I dropped by his home. He is a judge and we sat in his sun room reminiscing about good times. He offered me a cigar and I accepted. We had a wonderful conversation and I returned to the joy of cigars.

When I relocated to Cleveland, Ma Bell had me traveling the state. While making sales calls I went to a cigar shop, JoVann's Tobacco. It was a small shop located on SOM Center Road in the village of Mayfield Heights. They stocked a wide selection of cigars, pipes, pipe tobacco and other paraphernalia.

There were a few uncomfortable chairs to "park your ash." I'd buy a medium-priced cigar which was about three dollars and chat with Tony, the owner, and some of the regulars.

Monty, an older man who sold aluminum siding and wore big gold chains that looked like you could tow a car with them was usually there. One day while smoking a big cigar, he dropped dead. It was an interesting place. After nine years the store relocated nearby to a larger store.

JoVanns has been was my favorite local cigar shop for over 35 years. It's where I hang out and is frequented by many interesting people. The butcher, the baker, the candlestick maker live in this world and there is every shape, height, ethnic group, religion and color represented. The term "asshole" has become a form of endearment.

This is about an adult place where everybody does know your name. It is about grown men who sit around discussing the topics of the day with opinions. Old, young, gentile, Jew, black, white; a potpourri of people observing life.

We speak the philosophy of practicality while looking through the large windows facing a major road. You always see a reflection of yourself through the glass. It's a beautiful, sunny but brisk morning in Cleveland.

Tony, who is in his 80s, arrives at 9:30 to open. He is energetic and quick to express an opinion to anyone he meets. The regulars will soon arrive like men working shifts. He appreciates the customers and treats them well.

The coffee maker he filled starts brewing and he knows the first shift will be arriving. The shop was recently remodeled. Imagine six comfortable sofas placed in a circle facing Mayfield Road. He stares through the glass thinking who will be first.

If you enter through the back, on the left is a humidified room filled with large containers of mixed tobacco for pipe smokers. This is where Tony and his son Brent do the mixing and blending of pipe tobacco. There is a comfortable leather sofa where people can have meetings or use their computers and smart devices in private.

The coffee is almost done. It's free to any patron and next to the machine are, Styrofoam cups, cream and sugar. Some of the regulars bring ceramic cups. It's like home.

Moving toward the front of the shop, you pass a large humidified room that houses a huge selection of popular cigar brands: Perdomo, CAO, Oliva, Fuente, Henry Clay and many others. Because of the embargo, there are no Cuban cigars. They are illegal.

Prices range from $1 to $25 a stick (a term for one cigar) and there are natural (light) or maduro (dark) cigars. Most are handmade by a person called a "roller." A good cigar has a wrapper, more tobacco leaves and tobacco filler. The strengths are mild to full-bodied.

Cigars are made in the Dominican Republic, Honduras, Nicaragua, Mexico and Cuba. Many are made in Florida. When people fled Castro's Cuba, they brought their cigar making skills with them.

Tobacco products are stored in rooms or display cases where the humidity is kept between 65-70 per cent. This insures freshness. There also is a large humidor of pipe and cigarette tobacco. Many people roll their own cigarettes.

All the pipe tobacco has a tester jar in front of the blend. The consumer is welcomed to smoke a pipe full before making a purchase. With cigars you "buy 'em to try 'em!"

The first customer in the door asks about cigars and is told what to consider. Tony explains how to evaluate a cigar. You really need to smoke it to make an informed decision.

Many save the band which is around almost every cigar and tape it in a diary. A rating of 1-10, date smoked, taste, strength, size and price may also be noted. Over time it becomes an interesting book.

The Gilberto Cubana line is a private label made for Jovann's in either the Dominican Republic or

Nicaragua by Oliva, a large company. There are a variety of sizes and shapes. They sell for $3 to $6 each which is a medium-priced cigar. It is a good value for the money. Buying five gets you a discount and twenty, the best price.

As regulars arrive, the conversation starts. Golf and sports are popular topics. You'll hear about current events and, of course, children and grandchildren. "Whatever happened to..." begins a discussion about people who haven't been seen for a while. "You know who died…" will often kick off a dialog.

Most of the men are Democrats but there is little talk of politics. Nobody wants to offend. There are times when the discussion gets heated, yet we all remain friends.

Elmer and old Bill are normally the first "ancients" in the door. Time takes a toll on senior citizens and there are plenty that frequent the shop who are over the hill, me being one. Sid shuffles in and looks good for a man soon to be 95 years young. He always asks about my son. When I inquire about how he's doing, he doesn't complain but simply says, "Good for a man my age."

Sam is a professional salesman. His home improvement company does well and he says hello to everyone who comes in the shop. He has a great personality and is a good looking Italian-American.

His son Alex plays three sports: football, basketball, baseball and lettered in all three. His favorite is baseball. Today with the high cost of college, Sam is optimistic that he won't have to pay his son's way and hopes for an athletic scholarship. It would be a big help. I'm certain you understand.

Sam likes to bet on professional and college sports and claims he breaks even in the long run. He calls his bookie to bet on the Indians-Boston game.

Tony, a successful building contractor, was a championship wrestler in high school and works with young kids. He's middle-aged, has a winning attitude and serves as the chief troublemaker. He stirs the pot of controversy whenever things are in motion and says it's his job. He is blunt.

His favorite line is, "Let me tell you something," then he tells you. Experience in life, good parents and a great family has shaped him over the years. He loves to tell stories about his grandchildren and is a proud father. He'd do anything for you but you would have to ask. Among the regulars, he is the "Sheriff."

Attorney Bill, "Mr. Know it All," is talking sports, and asks who ran the first four-minute mile. Roger Bannister's name is mentioned. Bill confirms that it was "Dr." Roger Bannister.

He talks about his confirmation when he was sixteen. The rabbi who confirmed him was strict and old school. By answering a difficult question, Bill received a Torah blessing. You name the subject, person or event and he is in the discussion and has a memory for detail.

His kitchen remodeling project has been in motion for six months. It's being managed by our friend Tony, the general contractor. Living with a kitchen under construction is a challenge but the ordeal is nearly over. One of the new kitchen cabinets is lost on a truck. His wife wants new wood floors, so I give Bill a gift.

I've been a professional cleaner since 1980 and discovered a tremendous product used to clean floors after they are sanded and before they are sealed. Then the product is used for maintenance. I give him a bottle.

I told Bill the gift was conditional. He has to invite me to synagogue because I've never been to a Jewish service. I said if he liked the product, I'd give him refills for a cheap cigar. He said it would be a good cigar. I enjoy being a friend because he's smart and a good conversationalist.

John, a regular who hasn't been in for a long time, shows up. He quit cigars but decided to visit friends. I used to see him at the annual Geauga County Fair where he engaged visitors and promoted sales. When I ask, "Are you still working, Bill?" the attorney, interrupts and says, "Oh you didn't hear?"

I bought new appliances through John who sells for a major retailer: stove, microwave, dishwasher, refrigerator. He didn't sell service contracts for each product and a week later, with excellent sales numbers and high ratings for customer relations, he was fired. Our friend is over sixty, so you guess why.

Stan, an attorney who is one of the senior regulars, starts to discuss tennis. He still plays in a league, and smokes only Henry Clay cigars. He discourages anyone from trying the brand because he says he wants to corner the market. Everyone loves Stan who has a laid-back disposition. He is a sweet person and a committed Democrat. He always says, "You damn Republicans."

Stan died on December 23, 2013. He played tennis until the end, had a great demeanor and was 85 years old.

In the Jewish religion they have "Shiva" and for a period of seven days, the family of the deceased meet and reminisce with friends and family at the home of the dearly departed. One evening I met with Stan's spouse who welcomed me into her home.

I wore a sweater with a "Fender" guitar emblazoned in red on the front in honor of my friend who played oboe in the Army orchestra during World War II.

It isn't hard to talk about anyone over a bowl of good hot matzo ball soup and a slice of New York style cheesecake. If I hadn't eaten, I could hear Stan grumbling, "So my food's not good enough for you?" We will miss Stan who had many friends.

Roger works for Austin Powder, our local dynamite company and is a die-hard Republican. He was always talking politics with Stan and they would get into heated discussions. He was a serious gun collector. Smith & Wesson, Glock, concealed carry, and the National Rifle Association were often discussed. Roger disliked Democrats.

For years Stan and Roger were the odd couple at the shop. They were extreme opposites but best friends. Roger got Stan a membership in the National Rifle Association (NRA). In return Stan enrolled Roger in the American Civil Liberties Union (ACLU). Both are no longer with us and we assume they are sitting in the big cigar shop in the sky, arguing politics.

Will, the head of security for a school system, is constantly using his iPhone. If there is any question or dispute over facts; or you think out loud about anything, he immediately asks his phone. Yes, today many sane people talk to their mobile devices.

He is into weapons and loves to talk about guns, knives, bows, arrows and bullets. He is divorced but has a young girlfriend, also a divorcee. He says he is never getting married again. He sheepishly informed us that his girlfriend was pregnant. "What?" we say? "You've got to be kidding!" He got more crap from us than a chicken farm in a hurricane. Today, this shouldn't happen, we tell him. The regulars gave him a working over. It will all work out, says Will who is excited about his soon-to-be son. Yes, they know. We decide to have a baby shower for Will and his someday bride. We insist. After all, it has been a long time since he needed baby clothes. His son is fourteen. He can't argue, it's done. I offer him the use of a baby crib and he thanks me.

Ruby, whose first name is John, spends a lot of time at the shop. His adult son is a struggling actor trying to break into the movies. He is divorced and rarely turns down a free cigar. John attended the Castle Hill Military Academy in Tennessee. Bringing up a photo on his cell phone, he shows me a picture of two famous classmates. You may remember Duane and Greg Allman of the famous Allman Brothers Band. Their hits include: "Ramblin Man," "No One to Run With" and many more.

He served in the army and did tours in Germany and Viet Nam. He was a photographer for the *Stars and Stripes*, an army news publication. While traveling the world, he met such luminaries as Colin

102

Powell, Commanding General of the 5th Army (Secretary of State under President Clinton), and F. Lee Bailey, the famous attorney. His favorite recreation is snoozing, usually with a lit cigar in his mouth. Sometime we have to awaken him before he burns his shirt. He snaps to and says, "What?"

Everyone knows a person like Big Mike. When he arrives, the room is full of energy and everyone participates in his banter. He gives, takes and has all of us join in the conversation. Today, he talks about a smoker he attended at the VFW, a veterans club.

They hired two exotic dancers who decided to make a little extra money. After their act, they covered themselves with whipped cream. About 180 out of 200 men lined up and paid twenty dollars for the joy of having a lick. He swears he wasn't one of them. Mike talks about sports and is a high school enthusiast.

His friend Bill who we call Coach is active in the local sports world. Coach starts talking about days gone by and asks where I am from. I answer Youngstown. "I knew a guy who was a superb football player at Ohio State from there. His name is Gene Janecko and we were in the same fraternity." Gene is my cousin. I knew he was a good athlete but never realized great.

Coach, who is in his 80s, always travels with Big Mike. He is in top physical shape, has a sharp mind and recently returned from Florida. He intended to travel to Pasadena, California, for the Rose Bowl to watch Ohio State. They lost to Michigan and played in the Orange Bowl.

Mitch, one of our regulars, loves to curse. His favorite word (you can guess what it is) is used as a verb, noun, adjective, adverb and every other English form. He's a talker but nearly every sentence has to have a bad word. We all know people like this.

One morning six of us were sitting around talking about nothing. Charlie arrived and added to the mix. He can fall sound asleep in 20 seconds and sometime does. He loves to attend auctions and has been friends with the owner for many years. I suddenly realized that, at 70 years old, I was the youngest man in the group by ten years. Scary!

Elmer and his wife, Celia, celebrated 70 years of marriage on June 27. He comes from a wealthy family and was a musician. His best friend, Ray Anthony, had a famous big band in the 1940s. He played saxophone but never joined a traveling band. Being married, he needed to keep a regular job or who knows what he might have done in music.

Elmer went into business and did well. It's difficult for him to walk and he shouldn't drive, but every morning he arrives to smoke a cigar and complain.

Hey, someone shouts, I went to the Blossom Time Festival in Chagrin Falls to hear our friend Dave. He is talented; plays electric bass and sings in his cover band, Custard Pie. The music is from the late 60s and early 70s. He started the group years ago and says he'll hang it up when it's not fun anymore.

Dave knows that I've been a professional musician for over 50 years and also play electric bass. He is always asking me to sell my vintage 1962 Fender Precision bass because everything is original. Sorry!

Jim, who is in his early 40s, pops into the shop on a regular basis. He buys a few cigars and settles. He is shy and quiet. Years of suffering with mental problems dominate his personality. It's obvious that he is troubled. He likes big cigars and burns through them fast. After a few and a little banter, he departs.

Because I am bi-polar and suffer from depression, Jim and I usually have private talks about issues. He knows my mental history so we relate. Over the years, even though I am almost twice his age, we developed a friendship. He is a bachelor.

I received premium tickets to a Cleveland Indians baseball game and invited Jim, who was staying with his parents while his condo was being painted, to go.

When I picked him up, I sensed an uneasiness. He introduced me to his mother who I never met and she expressed concern. Jim said his grandfather left him a large trust fund and he had plenty of money, so I understood why she might have thoughts. She reminded him not to be late which was strange since it was a night game.

When we arrived at Jacobs Field, we parked and entered the Terrace Club. My benefactor gave me his membership card. The facility faces the field and you get a fabulous view of the field through glass.

We ordered dinner, watched batting practice and headed for our special seats before the game started. We were on the third base side, exactly two rows from the playing field and near the press dugout.

I spotted my good friend and professional photographer Ron Kuntz. A few years ago, Ron nearly won a Pulitzer Prize for an extraordinary shot of Indians catcher Sandy Alomar, sailing into a dugout upside down catching a foul ball.

"Hey, Ronnie!" I shout and we walk over to the press area. I introduce him to my friend Jim. "How about taking a photograph of us in our seats when the game starts?" Ron always obliges.

It was a beautiful night and we nearly caught a foul ball. Our primo seats dictated that we stay alert. I'm sure you've seen many a screamer smashed down the third base line into the seats. I asked him to send me an 8"x10" print which I later gave to Jim as a remembrance of a wonderful night.

Ron works as an independent contractor but for many years was employed by the Reuters News Agency. He died in 2013 at the age of 78.

Every now and then I would stop smoking cigars. My three to five a day habit was expensive. Good cigars range from three to ten or more dollars each. You do the math. However, I would always call my friend on our birthday, February 21, or send a card.

One year I did neither, so I picked up the phone and called to wish him a belated happy birthday. We agreed to meet at the shop, had had a great reunion and he brought me up to speed.

My friend struggles with depression and his wife died suddenly. His situation as a box salesperson deteriorated as he went from Salesperson of the Year to being shoved out the door by a new owner of the company he was with many years.

He is a cultivator and works smart. Unfortunately, in today's world, this is old school and why many age fifty-plus people can't get a job. They are beyond their field of endeavor, eventually become discouraged and give up. Middle age and older is tough to negotiate for men today. You are here (employed) today, gone (fired) tomorrow. You face age discrimination and hear you are overqualified. It can be depressing.

I arranged an interview for him with a box company that a friend of mine owns. It turned out to be good but the company couldn't afford him. I asked for some feedback so I might help and this is what many rejected job applicants, especially senior people, never hear.

First, he was a person with experience but too laid back. He didn't exhibit the fire and desire they wanted. Although he had many years of experience, his customer base was small. He wasn't aggressive, wanted too much and didn't bring enough. He was professional, maybe too professional. Today, middle agers everywhere are being given this message.

The regulars started arriving and there were new people. Dave, an Iraqi whose real name is Dawoud, loves to talk about "broads." He is intelligent and owns a limousine transport service but is aloof and always on defense. He is proud of his adult children. I have a standing breakfast, lunch or dinner invitation with him. I want to get behind the mask and get to know him better. He says never.

Harry shows up with a box of cannolis. Remember in the movie "The Godfather," when Clemenza says, "Leave the gun, take the cannolis"?

Lou is a graduate of USC and we talk about Xerox who he worked for in Palo Alto, California. I was with them for ten years. They had many thinkers who were paid by the "producers." The company wasted a fortune and projects like the Windows operating system were started and discontinued.

Other companies picked up pieces, continued development and made fortunes at the expense of Xerox's stupidity. Small, flexible, lean companies became giants. I saw laser technology in its infancy and they invented mammography which has saved many women by identifying breast cancer. I guess it's the American way.

Old Bill comes to the shop every day. He is a lonely widower who always sits in the same place and doesn't say much. When he speaks there is wisdom. He often reminiscences about the days when things were slower and better.

On Christmas, 2013, I awakened early and felt energized so I drove to the shop. Tony's longtime companion and high school sweetheart, Marianne, died while I was in Hawaii. He read me a poem he composed about their dormant and late blossoming love. It was heartfelt and beautiful. I asked if he wanted me to compose a song around the piece.

I went home, picked up my guitar and within an hour put music to the words. I slightly changed the lyrics and fell into a beautiful chord pattern. He said the shop would stay open until noon and I asked if he wanted me to come back and play the piece.

I arrived, entered the back of the shop and had a cup of coffee. I hadn't performed or played for five years. I started to sing and play for him but it turned out to be a rehearsal because the shop was busy and he was the only one working.

I moved to the front where we sit, waiting for Tony to get a break. The regulars: Attorney Bill, Guy, Sam, Charlie, Lou, Old Bill, John, and a few people I didn't know were there. Tony, the building contractor, held the music for me to read as I sang.

When I finished the tune (complete with a few minor mistakes), the place went silent. I had presented what Tony titled, "The Face of Love" to the group and everyone was moved.

It was a wonderful Christmas gift to give to a man who spent his life making friends, good friends at his shop. Though brusque at times, the one who we call "King Asshole" was teary eyed. He said, "Good job, asshole." I knew he appreciated it.

The regulars are some of the most interesting, intelligent and diverse men you will ever meet. Sometime women drop in, but it's rare. Attorneys, doctors, dentists, executives, salesmen from all walks,

110

politicians, sports figures, musicians and seasoned seniors who understand life. We have quite a cast.

Louie, a big Hungarian, walks by and steps on my toe. Ouch! He brought his black Pug dog, Swoozie, into the shop the other day. She is cute and maintains a good weight. I love Pugs. My dog, Pugsy, was a sweet beige female who was tremendous with children. She would jump up onto our bed, shimmy under the covers and sleep at our feet. What a wonderful foot warmer but she always snored. We got used to her symphony.

Lou is always asking people to join the Hungarian Club in Hiram, Ohio. I spring for the twenty dollar annual dues and plan to visit in the summer. They have weekend activities and special picnics. You pay five dollars to enter and there is food, music and adult drinks for sale at a reasonable charge. He said he'd pay for my first visit.

He loves Jeeps and usually does a signature burn out when leaving the shop. I recently ordered Hungarian Kolbas which is a sausage. It was the best I've ever eaten. Before Easter I'll receive my stuffed cabbage order and I know it will be good.

My friend Steve, who we call Cowboy is a technical product salesperson. He quit high school out of boredom but is a sharp professional, knowledgeable in his industry and well paid.

I started calling him Lippy because when he ate something brought to the shop (people are always bringing food and treats), he'd developed swollen lips. Something in the snack didn't agree with him. My wife is allergic to sesame seeds and breaks out in a rash if she eats one. His lips looked like balloons in minutes and gave a new meaning to the term "fat lips."

His latest sale to the railroad will earn him an ongoing commission. He mentions working on a medical robot and the doctors want a certain feature. If there is nothing in it for Steve, why bother. The idea sounds good and is feasible but he laments, "How would I make money?"

Never one without an idea or opinion, I suggest doing what Xerox Corporation did with their first plain paper copier, the 914. They rented it for a monthly fee and charged a nickel for every copy.

Put a meter on your idea and charge a fee per use. Steve ponders the solution but needs to determine if there is real interest. Throw a number at them, like $5000 per use and see if it goes from want to need. I expect a fine cigar, maybe even a box, since the idea could make him a lot of money.

If you've ever gone to a drive-in theater, you know it's fun. Today they are almost extinct. Steve invited me to meet him at the Mayfield Drive-in and guaranteed a great time. We sat in his car smoking fine cigars and listened to audio being sent by a radio signal. Steve listened through the car stereo and I had a headphone radio. The sound was great. This will be a regular event.

Guy works for a large insurance company and often swings by at lunch. He busts all of us and has a sense of humor. If anyone screws up and Guy hears about it, you can be sure he's going to ride you. We always greet him by saying, "Hi, Guy!"

He worked in radio at WWWE, WTAM and WHK, three powerhouses in the Cleveland market. Our mutual friend is Larry Morrow, a popular disc jockey who I've known thirty-five years. The radio business is a revolving door. Independents have been swallowed by the big operations like Clear Channel and almost everything is scripted.

TV is similar. In the past you had characters like Ernie Anderson who started a late night show, "Ghoulardi" featuring "B" horror movies. Ernie, a legend, is now deceased. He left Cleveland to join his pal, comedian Tim Conway (The Carol Burnett Show, McHale's Navy) in California and was the voice of ABC. He did voice over and became a hugely successful star in Hollywood.

Tim Conway, from Chagrin Falls, has benefitted the Chagrin Valley Little Theater and recently returned to have a reunion with many of his friends. He is humorous with an ability to ad lib and crack everyone up. He never forgot his hometown.

Michael, who lives nearby, sells insurance and is a Master Tailor. When I drop twenty-five more pounds, I'm going to have him make a blazer. His English Bulldog named Winston comes for visits. Michael and his dog are good listeners and we like them both. When you drive a Corvette, you expect a lot of razzing.

David, the artist in woodworking, creates products using exotic wood. Wearing a "Bubba Gump" shirt, he calls himself a Jewish shrimper. His business, Darbynwoods, focuses on creative and unusual products. He uses color from nature in everyday items. I recently had him craft a cigar cutter for me and the cutting mechanism is imbedded in a small oval piece of wood.

He makes a line of pens that range from $25-$115. I ask him to bring me few to evaluate. To a writer, the pen is a tool. Feel and balance facilitates creativity and I place an order. My pen will have a barrel made with olive wood from Israel, engraved with Mazel Tov, a star of David and November 4, 1974. Each represent a special time in my life.

I built a small recording studio in my home and David is aware of my guitar collection. We discuss ideas. He suggests some custom hangers with background slabs of rosewood, maple or cherry. I agree to email photos and he will give me ideas and cost estimates. It won't be cheap; it will be good.

Ron, the head of security for Cleveland State, is big, tall, has a nice demeanor and always engages. He has friends in many places. I usually meet him at the annual Cleveland State Jazz Festival. I admire his beautiful gold Rolex Submariner which is a watch that many of us only dream of owning. He smokes very fine and expensive cigars.

One of our favorite people is Doc. He is retired from dentistry and his wife Bonnie visits on occasion. She is a sweet person but has health issues. They travel and doc is a master at finding the "good deal." He is a friend to all.

Jimmy, a new fellow, started visiting on a regular basis. He was with Xerox for many years and retired. We have mutual friends and discuss former colleagues. I'll be able to reconnect, thanks to him.

Every men's group has a sports nut. Our expert is Silver who lives and dies with our Cleveland Indians, Browns and Cavaliers. It is always "next year" in Northeast Ohio and some of us are running out of time. Every Saturday, we listen to the same stories because seniors forget and Bill is 73. However, when it comes to sports statistics, ask Bill.

Since the Browns were returned to our city in 1999 they've been through eight coaches. The curse of Art Modell the owner who sold us to Baltimore, remains a negative. I feel sorry for my wife who is a huge sports fan. She makes me watch all the March Madness basketball games. I can hear many of you moaning with envy.

The Indians are owned by Larry Dolan, a wealthy man who lives in Geauga County. His son, Paul, is president of the team and baseball is important in Cleveland. The Indians are plagued by the "curse of Rocky Colovito" who was a god in the 1950s and traded for nobody. Cleveland fans are still bitter.

The team runs hot and cold but made it to the World Series in 1997. Carol and I, thanks to our son-in-law, Daryle, attended a game. He was head of marketing for the Indianapolis Indians (not related to our Cleveland team) and got us tickets. They were "nose bleed" seats but we were there. We sat next to his boss and it was a cold day. We dressed right and thanks to his extra hand warmers, we were comfortable. The Indians lost, of course.

David the "Mossman" is a native of Cleveland and WJW Fox 8 TV personality. He can be seen every weekday on "New Day Cleveland." His award-winning show is seen on Fox stations around the country.

He often drops in the cigar shop to enjoy our company. Recently he did a show from JoVann's on a day I was not there. Normally, it is a local interest story. He describes the business and chats with the owner and a few patrons. After the shoot, it's edited and he uses what fits.

David said our mutual friend, radio personality Larry Morrow, a force in Cleveland radio, was helpful to him when he was coming up in the business. I wasn't surprised. Larry, who I've known for years, is a wonderful person. He and his wife, Rosary, were responsible for getting us started in our business. He's made many friends over the years.

While I was deciding what to call this book my friend Bill, who always smokes a pipe when he visits, offered a suggestion. "Why don't you call it *Up in Smoke*?" Many of you may be familiar with the movie starring Cheech and Chong. This book has a totally different meaning and the title is often used. I decided it fit but added a subtitle. Thanks, Bill.

Finally, hitting in the cleanup spot, so to speak, is Hillbilly Joe, the garbage man. Like a piece of dropped paper, he blows in the door every now and then. He has a distinct drawl even though he's from Cleveland, and always needs a shave. He works as a driver for a major waste management company.

Sometime he brings treasure that he's picked up on his route: antiques, unopened boxes and valuables of all kind. Once he gave me a brand new bicycle for my youngest grandson which was placed at the curb with the trash. These days people dispose of everything and anything, like real life.

On February 7, 2004, George A. Peko, a young employee at the shop who was attending Cleveland State University composed the following:

"JoVann's Tobacco Shop is a place where many meaningful relationships have been developed. We have all made long lasting friendships, and even made new family members. JoVann's has given us memories that we will always cherish in our hearts. JoVann's may be a place where people come to buy tobacco, but for me and many others, JoVann's Tobacco Shop is home."

The sign hangs is a prominent place and below it, are individual photographs of the regular patrons including some who have departed.

JoVann's, is twenty miles from my home but I have a few options just in case. I live in the Northeast Ohio snowbelt and the roads can be difficult or impossible to drive in winter. My alternative hang out is Port Royal Tobacco, located in Solon. My friend Nick opened the store thirteen years ago.

He worked for JoVann's and Tony taught him the business so he decided to strike out on his own. Solon is a growing, thriving community and the demographics were right for a cigar store. His father, a retiree and also named Nick, helps during the week.

PR Cigar is next to the McDonalds in a strip mall. There is plenty of parking and the store is far enough from JoVann's that it does not directly compete. The two owners remain friends and I patronize both shops.

Nick, in his forties, is personable and a diehard Oakland Raiders football fan. He worries too much for a young man and it's taking a toll on his hairline. He treats his customers with respect and is quick to recommend a cigar if you need help. The store has a seating area near the sales counter with six comfortable chairs. The front of the store is all windows.

He always offers to cut your cigar and asks if you want a receipt. His selection is diverse and the glass counter in front showcases lighters, cigar humidors and miscellaneous things. In the back is a smoking room, "The Perdomo Cigar Lounge," with a big-screen TV, six leather sofas and a ventilation system.

Nick is divorced and his son is the apple of his eye. He closes on Sunday, normally a good sales day, to be with his boy. He's a Christian and we often speak about spiritual issues. We are both imperfect and our walk with God is by faith not by sight. Come on, we smoke cigars and have a beer every now and then!

Many of the customers at Nick's store live on their computers, smart devices and especially their mobile phones. Some wear a thing in their ear to constantly be in communication with who knows who.

A large walk-in humidor is in the middle of the store with a good selection of cigars. The most popular what I call "house cigar" is a line made by Perdomo and a good value for the money. Nick Perdomo is the owner of a large company and friends with Nick, the shop owner. The store features the Perdomo Cigar line. To further complicate things, my name is Nick. On occasion, when Perdomo visits. it is like the movie "My Big Fat Greek Wedding." Watch the DVD and you'll laugh. There is one scene where the father of the bride introduces Nick, Nick, Nick and Nick. After you watch it, think of PR Cigar. None of us are Greek.

The clientele is middle aged and a few seniors. Every cigar shop has its characters and PR is no different.

Tom is a gigantic Italian. His family has been in the decorative iron business for years. They are artisans with skills that command big dollars. He is a good conversationalist and friendly. If you want attractive iron work, call Tom but have deep pockets.

Doc Ray. who I know from JoVann's, is near retirement and says you work or you die. He was a regular at JoVann's but rarely visits his old haunt.

Tim owned a carpet cleaning company for ten years and now works for the Veterans Administration. We talk shop. I do high-end house cleaning and the subject turns to vacuum cleaners. I've used Windsor products for many years. He lights up and says, "It's what I use!" You'll see the Windsor line in hotels, hospitals and commercial accounts. They're pricey, about $600. Here is how I became hooked on them.

Jack, an old fashioned salesman with a company that I bought chemicals from, introduced me to my first Windsor. I was complaining that I always discovered a flaw after I bought a new machine. I contend that many products are designed by engineers who never use what they design. Think about your experiences.

Many sweepers are bulky, hard to control, break in the wrong spot and have short cords to name a few complaints. Jack said, "Our product is expensive but worth every penny. The next time you need a unit, I'll give you a demo to try for a week. Either bring it back or buy one." It became an easy sale.

When I bought my first unit, I wanted to see how much the bag would hold before the "change bag" light flashed. It was typical German engineering. The bag was completely filled to the top and still maintained good suction. In fifteen years, I've never replaced a belt in my seven machines.

Pat, an attorney and friend for many years, is a wild man. He smokes OpusX, an expensive cigar, and is watching a TV show about racing. He is short. Usually short people smoke big cigars, and Pat and I fit the profile. He has a big personality, loud voice, is a character and loves fast cars. I meet him at JoVann's on occasion. Pat lives in the fast lane and loves life. Recently he was bragging about a trip to Hong Kong. I asked if he liked China. He said he didn't go to China. The last time I checked, the city was still part of the Republic of China.

Some of the other guys are on their cell phones and smart phones but the atmosphere is one of total relaxation.

Jason, an engineer, talks about the youth, especially blacks since he is African-American. I mention the trades. Plumbing is what I'm encouraging my grandchildren to learn. You can make over $100,000 a year and your tools fall off at 5 p.m. When you want a plumber after hours they charge a fortune and if they don't want to work they say call someone else. That is independence.

Lenny walks into the shop. He is a suave, well spoken, well-dressed friend who visits both JoVann's and Port Royal. He owns race horses and his computer consulting company does well. We talk about sports. The Cleveland Browns are searching for another coach. I tell Lenny he should be in the movies.

I never bought into any device that controls your life. My hello and good-bye flip phone served me well for many years. I recently activated my voice mail and started carrying my mobile device. I am not a heart doctor or brain surgeon, so no life or death will hang in the balance because I can't be contacted. Later works for me.

I upgraded to an iPhone and went to school for instructions. I still depend on my grandchildren for help. If you get a call from me at a weird hour it's because my finger slipped.

Roger, a regional sales representative for the Perdomo Cigar Company, is having a promotion. He exhibits his product line next to the front counter but looks tired. Last night he returned from Nicaragua where he stayed at a guest home that Nick Perdomo owns. One patron asks for information and Roger helps him.

We talk about my book and music. His father is 90 years old and plays harmonica. I buy a box of cigars. They are pricey but today you get a discount and some goodies. I get a beautiful ash tray and four Perdomo Connecticut wrapped cigars as a reward.

Roger agrees to review part of my unpublished book and call it to Nick's attention. Maybe the world-wide company will consider using *Up With Smoke* as a promotional tool. This would be a big break. They could sponsor me and pay in fine cigars.

Most of us realize that the only thing constant is change. We all have to deal with it and so it goes with me. Over time my old hangout has gone through change and it was time to move on.

Did you ever have a friend who constantly invites you to visit a place and you keep putting it off? My friend Ed was always asking me to visit his cigar lounge. He is a character who loves his Jeep, enjoys radio-controlled cars and has a concealed carry permit. Smith & Wesson, his two best friends, are often by his side. I finally traveled with him to his favorite haunt.

Royal Havana Cigars in Willoughby, Ohio, is housed in a historical one-story building. The shop is a throwback to the 50s and 60s. Everything is old-time comfortable and the setting is relaxing. Five antique couches and many artifacts from that era are tastefully placed. The lamps are basic 50s style.

Do you remember big round coffee tables? Two of them are used to create specific areas. The walls are adorned with reminders of the past and create a warm atmosphere.

One wall has a framed blow up of a beautiful photograph of old Havana, Cuba. It's about 48 inches by 60 inches and makes you feel like you are there. Dave, the owner, took the shot when he lived in Cuba. He was raised in the Euclid, Ohio, area and his grandparents came from Slovenia. He graduated from Lake Catholic High school and Lakeland Community College. While considering a four-year college, he decided to move to Los Angeles and entered Pepperdine University. After graduation, he became a successful stock broker with his own TV show. He was in California but his heart was in Cuba.

His brother Dan went there in 1994 to produce a sports documentary about Cuban boxers. Dave went for a visit, remained for many years and married a Cuban girl. Teofilo Stevenson, the legendary amateur boxer who won the 1972 Olympics, was his best man. Dan recently wrote an article for *Cigar Aficionado*, a popular cigar magazine which will appear in the fall (2014) issue.

As in all communist countries, there are controls and restrictions. His wife was pregnant with twins which created a problem. The young couple fled Cuba to start a family in the US. They returned to Ohio.

Dave was selling insurance and hating every minute. While having lunch with his sister, Roseanne, he spotted a vacant building. He thought it would be a great location for a doughnut shop or a cigar lounge. It started him thinking.

His former wife was a cigar roller in Cuba so he knew the business. He spoke fluent Spanish, had many contacts in the tobacco industry and was always interested in cigars. It became an easy decision.

Royal Havana Cigars (RHC) opened in 2012 with little fanfare. The store is large. There is a humidified room filled with many boutique brands, including his private label. Free coffee is always available and there are regular patrons who frequent the shop.

RHC has its own "app" that can be added to your smart phone. You receive regular notices of events and are automatically notified when you are in the area. Dave's main marketing tool is his friendliness. You immediately feel at home when greeted.

All purchases can be recorded to your account when you sign up for the app. This makes you eligible for discounts. For every ten cigars you purchase you receive one free. Events are normal: cookouts, picnics, golf outings, cigar rolling days, pig roasts and interesting things for the customers.

Tony, one of his part-time employees, is an old friend who lives nearby. We often chat about our times at other places we've frequented. His friendly personality and boyish smile makes you comfortable.

Like every hangout, there is a diverse group of regulars who I am meeting. Phil, his accountant, helps out and Adrian, one of his good friends, is president of The Great Lakes Cigar Club.

Adrian, now serves as my promotions and marketing advisor and plans to shoot a video of me being interviewed. He'll put it on Facebook and YouTube. He also arranged a few newspaper interviews which will give me and the book exposure. I also have some speaking events.

Dave gave me the title of "Author in Residence" and said that one day there will be a bust of me located in a prominent place. Don't I wish!

Shades of Earnest Hemingway, the famous author. He was renowned for novels like *The Sun Also Rises, A Farewell to Arms, For Whom the Bell Tolls* and *The Old Man and the Sea*, which won the 1953 Pulitzer. In 1954, Hemingway won the Nobel Prize.

His favorite haunt was Sloppy Joe's, a bar located in Key West, Florida, where he did some writing.

I had my first publicized book signing at Royal Havana Cigars and for a few hours felt like a star. Shaking hands, chatting with strangers and signing autographs was easy to do.

Dave just returned from a week in Cuba and the event was filled with energy. It was a big deal for me. I also meet Dave's twin sons, Darius and Daniel. They politely greeted me as I entered Royal Havana Cigars to do some writing.

I'm also greeted by Kenny, a gourmet chef. His day job as operations director for a major corporation keeps him busy. The first time we met I declined to taste a dish that he prepared. Fortunately for me, I tried one of his killer cheeseburgers at a later date. I was hungry and the burger was one of the best I've ever eaten. I promised Ken that I would never (a word I seldom use) refuse to taste anything he made. Ken loves to cook.

During my book signing, Kenny and his wife Melanie were an active part of the evening. She is charming and a fun person. It's not often that wives accompany their husbands to a cigar shop.

AJ, who traveled with Dave to Cuba, starts discussing the trip and describing the experience. They had a lot of fun and little sleep. He is from the Cleveland area and was a policeman for 27 years. After getting his law degree he eventually became a judge. He is usually very reserved and a man of few words. Tonight he was a wellspring of stories and laughs. I'm sure he'll return to Cuba and visit his adopted son. I'm not kidding and he has papers to prove it.

Guido, a retired Marine, talks about military life and how service members maintain a network of friends for life. Traveling the world as he's done makes for great conversation.

He recently visited the Tre Sorello boutique which means three sisters. Christina owns the shop and her father Joe is a new friend of mine. It is located in the Little Italy section of Cleveland and specializes in one of a kind merchandise.

His wife Ruth spent $2,200 dollars during the visit and they loved the place. The women's clothes she carries are unique and come from many places throughout the world.

Joe, Christina's father, is a character and a personable marketeer. He sold heavy equipment and his latest passion is putting together cigar events at upscale locations. During our first meeting, he had me mesmerized for a few hours as he discussed his interesting life. He was raised in the Little Italy section of Cleveland where he owns property.

We met at Cafe' Michael in Bainbridge, owned by our mutual friend Jamie. He said Joe was someone I should meet. Jamie was 101st Airborne and Joe is a former Marine. Both are cigar smokers.

We hit it off and Joe is planning to have an event at the restaurant. He tells Jamie, we'll get a big tent and you will barbecue. There will be a large Army vehicle parked in your parking lot and Nick will be autographing his book.

My "cigar girls" will sell cigars. Books and food will be included in the event price. Joe says that one of his girls made $500 in tips at the last event and everything is on the up and up. No "hanky panky,"

I recently attended an event sponsored by Perdomo Cigars at the Royal 10 cigar shop in North Royalton, Ohio. Royal Havana Cigars has a product line and these friends of Dave carry it.

Dave gave me a message to give to Steve, one of the partners. I passed the information on and Steve gave me a reply for Dave. Being a messenger between a Slovenian and a Greek can be dangerous. Here is the message and the response. I said to Steve, "The rum will come." His reply, "Get me two cases instead of one." I've sampled this rum and it's the best. Other than this, I know nothing.

I presented a copy of my book to my friend Roger, their regional representative and young Nick Perdomo who was traveling with Roger. Of course his future will be with the family company.

Nick said he would be sure to get *Up in Smoke* in the hands of his father. I'm excited as I think about what could happen.

When you are in northeast Ohio you may find me at Royal Havana Cigars in Willoughby. If you contact me ahead of time, I'd be happy to greet you. I love meeting new people and pride myself on being a good listener.

If you arrive unannounced, ask Vince, Tommy, Tony, Mike, Rick, Daniel, Bob, Sam, Al, Craig, his sister Joyce or any of my new friends if I'm expected.

You are only a stranger once at Royal Havana Cigars so stop on by. Their web site is: www.royalhavanacigars.com

Roaming

Think of things you did if you've ever been desperate. When age becomes a factor, good jobs are scarce. The challenge is to press on.

Selling AT&T alarm systems on straight commission, with no benefits, isn't really a job. Sometime you have to take a chance. The company said they provided leads. Most of mine were bad and only added mileage to my car but it was there that I met Rick, a geeky looking guy who became a friend. We both quit on the same day.

Cable TV was becoming popular and Viacom was looking for sales people. I'd never done door-to-door selling because I thought it was the lowest rung on the sales ladder.

When you are unemployed and probably unemployable, you start thinking differently. I got an interview with the sales manager who said the job was simple. You arrived for work at three in the afternoon, received an area to work and hit the road. You sold until dark or when people wouldn't let you into their homes.

The cable company hired anybody who could speak, write an order and was willing to work. It was straight commission; no advances, guarantees, draws or benefits. What you sold for the week was paid the next week. If you made your quota you were eligible for a full tank of gasoline. Every Thursday you were given a new area and some leads.

Sonny Geraci, the former lead singer of The Outsiders was a salesman and completely out of music. He was a top producer and agreed to train me. You drove your personal vehicle but on my first day I rode with Sonny to observe his technique.

If you ever saw him do a show, you know he is handsome with a warm, outgoing personality and much charisma. He was successful selling cable because he knew how to close. We started early and worked late.

One of the tricks he taught me was how to get into a high-rise apartment after dark when homeowners wouldn't let you in the door. Once you entered a complex, it was like shooting fish in a barrel. Prospects were home and usually answered a knock on the door. Also, you didn't need to deal with rain, cold or snow. Geraci had a great pitch.

Most sales people drove small or medium size cars except on gas bonus day. Then you would see Cadillacs, big station wagons, huge Oldsmobiles, Buicks and some trucks which were not popular like today. Usually they were low on fuel. I remember helping a guy push his out of gas automobile to the pump. I wondered where those cars came from.

A few years later Sonny, who had a few big hit records, started a band. TJ Lubinsky from Pittsburg started producing Oldies and Doo Wop shows for PBS which became a huge success and re-started the careers of many former stars. After we both moved on from cable sales, I met Sonny and asked how things were going. Thanks to this revival, he was traveling and appearing in oldies shows. Sonny said they send a round-trip plane ticket, pick him up (usually in a limousine) and drive him to the gig. He sings a few songs, gets a check that doesn't bounce and catches a plane home.

Blossom Time in Chagrin Falls is an annual festival and I went to hear him sing. He was planning to move to California, closer to his three children, who are trying to get into the music business. Being there would make him more effective in helping them. He has a name, a few hit songs, contacts and professional credentials.

In April 2012, he suffered a brain aneurism and was flown back to Cleveland to have several operations. He remained in Ohio and needs to use a wheelchair. There is hope that physical therapy will help. His memory and speech is clear and as usual his attitude is positive.

Many of his famous friends held a local fundraiser. Sonny always had a beautiful, gentle and sincere personality who everyone, including his peers, loved.

I was able to spend time with him at the show but he is frail. His performing days are over.

In the late 70s, I had an office in downtown Chagrin Falls as the guest of a friend I knew from church. He graduated from the University of Pennsylvania Wharton School of Finance. His partner, a computer programming genius, graduated from Princeton. This was a time when home energy efficiency and electricity use was a popular issue with utility companies.

Bill started the company and John was marketing and sales. Their product was a computer program on the Boeing Computer Network which was accessed via a hand-held computer.

The field technicians at numerous electric companies would take measurements at a home, download the results and the program did its calculations. The analyst printed a report at the home that showed energy utilization and suggested how to reduce costs.

My friends were paid a royalty on every audit and received a check every month. I was trying to decide my life's work. Since they didn't charge me rent, my only expense was a phone. This was a place to hide and act like a real business. It was a bad time for me mentally. I had gone through many jobs and my confidence was low.

I couldn't decide if I was a sales trainer, marketing person, salesperson or writer. I collected unemployment compensation and was sliding into debt.

Bill taught me how to use one of the first Apple computers and John discussed finance and marketing. I learned computer applications such as word processing but did no programming. I had nothing to do with their company, but my physical presence kept them from arguing.

The money was pouring in for them and both were alcoholics. Bill was quiet and would mentally disappear in the middle of a conversation. He was never without a cup of what I thought was coffee. He would work around the clock to maintain and update their energy audit program. John was lazy and they ended up despising each other.

Bill decided to develop a billing system for dentists because his good friend allowed him to use his practice as a model for the program. He soon had a useable billing system. It was a bundled package: hardware, software, training and support. I agreed to sell as an independent contractor and also trained the customer on how to use the product.

The office relocated from Chagrin Square to a larger facility and John stopped showing up except to get his monthly check. He had nothing to do with the dental system. Bill lamented about the fact that they were equal partners and didn't have a buy-sell agreement. He was stuck but honored the mistake by continuing to split the profit fifty-fifty.

John divorced his wife and I rarely saw him. He was always living large, drinking, chasing women and driving his Corvette. He died in his early sixties.

Bill continued with the businesses and the booze. I remained with him even though he became reclusive and continued to sell the dental system. Then Bill died. They were both good to me and another era of my life ended. I moved my furniture home and called it a day. I was unemployed, again.

Rick, my friend from the burglar alarm days, contacted me and said he was selling framed art. The lithographs were cheap, sold easily and he was making good money. Every day he went to a warehouse in Cleveland, picked up product then went anywhere he wanted, making cold calls in the business community.

You walked in unannounced carrying a stack of pictures and said, "What do you think about these?" The framed lithographs were shown to the first person seen and you waited for a reaction. They sold easily. At the end of the day you reported back to the warehouse with your money (you also could take credit cards) and settled up. The art sold for $20 and you made $10.

Did you ever know someone high strung who would explode over nothing? I went to the warehouse and mentioned Rick. The owner was a nut and within three sentences threw me out of the place. Mark and I didn't hit it off.

I needed a job and knew I could do well so I returned and begged for a chance. He weakened which was easy because he made a profit on every sale with no investment. I bore all the risk and the company shared the reward. For Mark, it was a no brainer; for me, it became a great opportunity.

JR, my trainer, taught me the basics. He was in the process of having a sex change and receiving psychological counseling to help him deal with his new life as a woman. It was the strangest situation I ever encountered in my life.

Soon, I had more sales than everybody because I was relentless, went into every business and knew how to close. I'm organized and developed a system to be more effective. In the morning I'd load my car with product and use a luggage cart to roll in more art than one could carry.

Mark made me the sales manager and gave me an override on every sale. I still went selling after my people left. The company decided to take the top producers on a three-day vacation to Jamaica. JR, my trainer, made the trip. He asked us to call him "Suzanne" and experienced the trip as a woman. It was weird and my wife was shocked.

On a snowy night, I was returning from a visit to Youngstown with a car full of art work. I crossed a bridge over a reservoir and hit black ice. My small car went into a spin, out of control and I slammed into a guard rail. The rest is a blank.

I was walking along the road in shock when a Marine in dress blues returning from the Marine Ball stopped to help. He had a cell phone to call the auto club. They towed my car to my mechanic. Then drove me to the Geauga Hospital Emergency Room.

I had my seat belt on or I would have been killed. My neck was swollen like a balloon but nothing was broken. The hospital wanted to hold me overnight but I insisted on leaving. I had no hospitalization coverage. Carol was away and my daughter came to get me.

I had an art show scheduled the next day and did it sporting a huge neck with black and blue bruises everywhere. I didn't sell one picture. A few days later I went to see my car. My mechanic had it towed to the junk yard and said I was lucky to be alive. The swelling ended and so did my career selling pictures.

My grandiose idea was to start an art sales business which I called "Art on the Cart." I drove to New York City, met with a company that made framed art and placed my initial order. Then I rented office space and a small warehouse, bought furniture, ordered phones and hired some telemarketers. In a stupid moment, I bought a used tow motor to move and stack product and paid for everything on a credit card. I also leased a new car.

I hired Bill, an unemployed friend who couldn't find a job, as controller. CJ, a high energy friend with a big personality, became the sales manager. He needed five thousand dollars so I used another credit card to make him a loan. You know how handy and painless those credit cards can be. He was a con man, never repaid the loan and the whole thing cratered after six months leaving me deep in debt and depressed. I was a sick man.

I decided to try to get another business going and went deeper into debt. Finally, I became so depressed I couldn't get out of my pajamas or my bedroom. At the lowest point, I couldn't open the drapes and wouldn't speak to anyone. I slipped further into depression and was out of control.

I've struggled with fear and insecurity since I was a child. Insanity was something no one talked about, like divorce. I felt I had to end it somehow. I couldn't take any more. Nothing worked and the outlook was grim. Suicide seemed to be the answer.

I was a "born again, evangelical Christian," but couldn't stand myself. I had three children and a wonderful spouse. They deserved better than what I was providing. When would be the right time? My businesses failed and so had I. To make some money I was playing bass in a Slovenian polka band but hated myself. I managed to avoid alcohol.

We were in jeopardy and heading toward disaster. I typically would put the cart before the horse. First, I'd dream a scheme that made sense, write a business plan and borrow money to get everything in place; then came the selling which never seemed to work out. I was lower than whale poop which is on the bottom of the ocean.

Everyone in Cleveland knew Larry Morrow, a popular disc jockey. We attended a Bible study in 1979 when my office with the phone company was downtown. He lives three miles from me and one morning while having breakfast at Joey's, a Chagrin Falls restaurant, Larry and his wife arrived.

I asked them to join me and we started talking. Rosary was looking for someone to help with ironing and cleaning a few days a month. I said Carol might be interested. The two met and Carol started.

Shortly afterward, John and Terri, two wealthy friends of Larry's, said they were looking for a housecleaner. This was the start of a new adventure but I didn't realize it yet.

I remember the day Carol drove me to Windsor Hospital, a mental institution in Chagrin Falls. It was the saddest day of our married lives. Carol loved me and was devastated. I needed help. I hated every moment of the stay, but had to get out for the weekend to play music.

I was fearful, frustrated and believed the end was near. It wasn't a very good witness for a Christian. The hospital put me on Prozac which helped and I lost some weight. The most horrible moment came when a couple who I knew from music showed up to visit their friend. They spotted me and I was embarrassed. I was released for the weekend to play music.

At the time we attended Garfield Memorial United Methodist Church and had no hospitalization coverage. One of the members of the church was the Director of Psychiatry at the renowned University Hospital. Carol spoke to the Pastor and arranged for me to meet the doctor and he agreed to help. My treatment plan required a $10 copay per visit and there would be a charge for medication. I starting meeting with the psychiatric staff at UH once a week. They diagnosed me as severely depressed and bi-polar. For over a year I received wonderful care and was never charged. I think the church paid the bills.

I got better but realized my illness had been with me my whole life. I was born premature and made up for it by being fat. I was called "fatty-fatty," "two by four" and "fatso" during my grade school years. It kept me down.

I was a problem child in school. Throughout the lower grades, I had to sit next to my teacher's desk. I felt ridiculed and unloved. During school functions the principal referred to me as "Spanky" of "Little Rascals" fame. It embarrassed me and I didn't like the reference.

I dealt with my insecurity by being the first student to arrive at grade school. I'd talk with the two janitors and station myself at the front door. I was starved for attention and had low self-esteem. I appointed myself the official door opener. When teachers arrived, I would greet them with a firm and cheery "good morning." This always brought a positive comment from them and comforted me.

This problem manifested itself in a significant way when I became a young adult. Eventually I became an egomaniac with an inferiority complex. Later, my training at Xerox convinced me that I made things happen and I became an angry and aggressive.

Morbid obesity and suicidal thoughts are not good. I looked like a slob and was planning to kill myself. I had a very thick rope and knew where I could attach it in the garage so nothing would break. The time was near. I just couldn't take any more. I didn't feel well, was broke and deep in debt.

Even though I was a "born again, evangelical Christian," I couldn't stand myself. I also quit going to church. I had three children, and a wonderful spouse, and they deserved better than what I was providing. When would be the right time to end it?

I was out of work, and unable to land a job so I started going with Carol to help her clean. This is something I was good at because I spent every Saturday as a boy, cleaning my mother's home. She was the "Queen of Clean." I dusted, vacuumed, scrubbed the bathroom and washed all the windows.

Mother would check my work before I was allowed to go out to play. She was brutal. If there was one thing wrong, I had to do the whole house again. I became efficient and thorough. Who wanted to do things twice? I never dreamed this skill would benefit me.

Carol started getting more customers and everyone said we should start a cleaning business. We also filed for Chapter 13 bankruptcy to keep our home.

I began cleaning windows and landed a few commercial accounts to do at night. All the business was gained by referrals and were within fifteen miles of our home. Something worked because we're still in business after thirty-five years

Our appeal was to the high end of the market. Money is always an object so I developed a matrix that listed all competitors pricing. I updated it twice a year and knew in detail what residential cleaners were charging.

I knew how to sell, when to walk away and how to say it's not for us. We are now winding down and the end is near for many things.

We enjoy today. You can't change yesterday and hope there will be a tomorrow which for a Christian is guaranteed. We walk by faith and not by sight.

It's a wonderful life. This morning I said, "How are you doing?" to an old timer at my favorite coffee shop. He cheerfully retorted, "I'm the oldest person in my Yoga class and living the good life."

Photos and Music

I first met Ron Kuntz when he spoke at a Christian men's organization years ago. He is a strong, dedicated believer and deeply involved in the "Champions for Life" ministry which was started by football great, Bill Glass. Bill played on the 1964 Cleveland Browns team which won the NFL championship.

The ministry is aimed at youth and the imprisoned. Ron is an active participant in the ministry. He not only shares the gospel of Jesus Christ but also handles the photography needs of the organization.

He contacted me and said that the group was planning a two-day event in the Cleveland area. This would be a prison outreach and they are always looking for Christian volunteers to serve as counselors. He asked if I would like to be involved and I couldn't say no. I've participated in many Bible studies but had never done anything like this.

Teams of men would visit two prisons, the Cleveland women prison and another prison south of Cleveland. I would attend a brief mandatory training program prior to the event.

Visiting prison is an unnerving experience. There are strict rules that must be followed and you are totally under the control of the guards from the minute you enter the property until you leave. The wrong action or comment can result in immediate removal.

I was Ron's helper for the two days that we ministered. He spoke, individually and collectively, to many of the inmates as a featured speaker and also served as the official photographer. Ron is generous with his time and has a great love of Jesus Christ and people, especially the incarcerated. He shares the Gospel through his own testimony and the love he exhibits to everyone. Ron only has friends because he is a friend to all.

It was a great experience. On the last night, I attended a banquet the ministry had for volunteers. Bill Glass and many other celebrities spoke words of thanks and encouragement to us.

Over the years, Ron has traveled all over the world. He's photographed and become friends with a host of famous people. In his book *A Cleveland Original: 50 Years Behind the Lens*, you'll see interesting photos of heavyweight champ Muhammad Ali, Hall of Fame pitcher and Cleveland's own Bob Feller, basketball star Michael Jordan and more. My personal favorite (on page 21 of Ron's book) is comedian Jonathan Winters. Many current greats like Robin Williams and other comedians cite Winters as a great force in their development and successful careers.

Years ago while visiting his home he started showing me his many photographs. Each had a great story because Ron is a character. When we came to a photo of him in his Australian bush hat and comedian Jonathan Winters in a Cleveland Indians uniform, I said, "Ronnie, I need a copy of that photo!" I mentioned that I often refer to myself as the illegitimate son of Jonathan Winters. I am a dead ringer. I have been approached by strangers asking me and my children if I am that comedian.

Ron has taken some of my favorite photos at the stadium. I have one with my grandson, Nicholas, during a promotion where we are wearing the same baseball caps. We leaned over the end of the press dug out, our faces side by side and Ron took a shot. It is a wonderful picture. Nicholas was ten and a fellow photographer handed him a game ball. Wouldn't you be thrilled?

I have some wonderful photos with my sweetheart who loves sports. She is a rabid Indians and Browns fan and understands the intricacies of sports.

While sitting outside Panera's in Bainbridge having a coffee, I struck up a conversation with Paul, a cellist with the Cleveland Orchestra. He is from Rhode Island and lives in the area. We talked about Oberlin College and his experiences in the music world. Paul met Dave Brubeck waiting for a flight at the Cleveland airport. He knew Dave's son, also a cellist.

We talked about Danny Kay, the actor, who is also an accomplished musician. I related some of my experiences over my years in music.

I called my friend when I read an article about the orchestra performing in Miami and Naples, Florida, in February. They appeared at a private party hosted by Donald Trump at the Mia Largo estate. The attendees were decked out in fur, gloves and hats. They were freezing.

When I was a young man working in Virginia, I wore only a sweater in winter. Everyone thought I was crazy but to a Northerner, sixty degrees is cool.

Paul said, "We'll discuss the party when I return," and said Trump is a one-way conversationalist. He talks, you listen. I refer to this phenomenon as "voice rapture." It is when you can't hear enough of yourself. Many in radio suffer from this affliction.

Stan Kenton, the legendary jazz pianist and band leader, was the first famous musician I ever met personally. I was introduced to him in 1962 by his friend, Eddie, who managed the Elms Ballroom where Stan came to do a show. He was an encourager and his autographed picture to me hangs on the wall of my office. It has great meaning.

I saw Tony Bennett do a show in Washington DC, and we met after the show. A few years later I was visiting the "Latin Casino" in Cherry Hill, New

Jersey, during a job interview and we met again. He had tremendous charisma, a great voice, and a skilled pianist who was his accompanist, Ralph Sharon. Everyone still loves Bennett.

I first met Buddy Rich at the Packard Music Hall, in Warren, Ohio. I was backstage talking to him when he was served divorce papers. I comforted him by listening to his ranting and raving, It was something he never forgot; not the divorce, but me.

Years later I was working for Xerox in Rochester, New York, and Buddy came to town to do a show at a nearby restaurant. Xerox Square is a twenty-nine story office building connected to a mall. The restaurant was in the mall and I stopped for lunch.

I noticed Buddy eating alone. I knew he was high strung and appreciated privacy. He was known to be brutal toward fans who disturbed him and would dismiss people who irritated him with a nasty word. I approached while he was eating and introduced myself by reminding him of Warren, Ohio, and a not so wonderful time, his divorce papers.

He remembered and invited me to have lunch with him. I made a dinner reservation for my wife and I for that evening. I remember saying I'd appreciate a good seat. When we arrived, our table was next to the stage, ten feet from the master of the drums.

Buddy always did a great show and surrounded himself with the best musicians. He is recognized as one of the best drummers in the world and had the fastest hand speed of any drummer who ever lived.

He is witty, had a cutting sense of humor and could have been a comedian. He was always funny when appearing on the Johnny Carson Show and put on a drum clinic that night, one I will always remember.

Northeast Ohio is a hotbed of musical talent. The Dana School of Music at Youngstown State University is well known and respected. They sponsored a "Night with Count Basie" at Stambaugh Auditorium. I met the Count---whose first name is Bill!---before the performance. He was playing poker and you never disturbed him during a card game, his manager told me.

I also met Joe Williams, a legendary vocalist who was performing with Basie. We spent time talking after the show. These two men and some of the other greats I've met are in the history books of music.

Jack Jones was a favorite of my sister-in-law, Michelle. She loved him. He booked Stambaugh Auditorium so I purchased an extra ticket and invited her to be my guest. She was thrilled. Road shows would often book Youngstown because it is midway between Pittsburgh, and Cleveland. It usually was an easy gig and you made a few extra bucks. Remember this was back in the day.

We arrived early and took our seats expecting a good show. Jack did a forty-five minute set, no encore and left the building. I was steamed because Michelle and all attendees deserved more. He gave us the short shrift. I never again listened to him or bought his music.

Peter, Paul & Mary were hired as the featured act during my senior year in college. Youngstown University did not have a large auditorium so they rented the nearby Struthers Field House. This was in the late 1960s when they were new, fresh and at the top of their game. It was a wonderful show and the place was packed. They became legends.

Big D. Irwin was a large, jovial singer who had one hit. His rendition of "Would You Like to Swing on a Star" would light up an audience like you wouldn't believe. I did a show with him at Idora Park on WHOT day in the early sixties. The Tokens, who sang "The Lion Sleeps Tonight" were also a featured act at Idora. They were typical New Yorkers and we upstaged them.

Link Wray, inventor of the "power chord," and his Ray Men were promoting their instrumental, "Rumble" and on route to a gig. They briefly popped into the Elms when the Del Rays were playing. They arrived late pulling a small trailer full of equipment. We laughed when the organ player carried in his instrument with a bear hug of a grip by himself. Link played two songs, packed and left.

Chuck Mangione, a great trumpet player who had a big instrumental hit, "Grazin' in the Grass," was always to be seen at Xerox Square when I lived in Rochester. We'd say hello as we passed but I never had a long conversation with him. The Mangione brothers are respected musicians in the city that is home to the Eastman School of Music.

The Del Rays did two shows with The Crystals in Akron when they were on tour promoting their hit records. We backed them up and did our own thing.

Del Sinchak & the Saints were a popular polka band in the Youngstown area. Every ethnic group had their halls and camp grounds. Del is Slovak and filled many places with music for hard working people from Eastern Europe.

Usually people who are foreign still love the old country. In their homes and farms they make ethnic food: pierogi, roasted lamb and pig, stuffed cabbage, kolbas, strudel, polenta and bread. There is beer, liqueurs and music. I've known many of these people.

Before music became a profession, I listened to Corky and the Bottle Caps and wished I had a band.

Corky played guitar and sang. Herb, who had some front teeth missing, played bass. My classmate John played sax and they had a drummer. They were stars to me and played at small parties usually for a minimal charge, free food and drinks.

Mike Roncone, a well-known musician, and his band were regulars at the best clubs. He played a Gibson guitar and sang. He was a great chord player but didn't play a lot of lead. He fronted one of the most popular Youngstown bands in the 1960s. We became friends.

Dick Nard and the Imperials were a rock group that I appeared with for a few years after the breakup of the Del Rays. Dick was a good sax player and nice guy. His drummer, Jack, had one of the first great car stereo systems. After practice, we'd sit in the automobile and listen to the radio.

I've known a few musicians from the area who had a taste of fame. Dick was working the midway at Idora Park when the Del Rays were in their prime. He idolized the band and later started a group called the Human Beingz. Their re-recorded version of the Isaly Brothers hit song "Nobody but Me" became a hit for them and is still played on the radio.

Daniel Pecchio, a bass player, also loved our band and played in Glass Harp. John Sfarra played drums and guitar virtuoso Phil Keaggy became a famous

154

Christian recording artist. Daniel lives near me and was also with the Michael Stanley Band who were regional stars. I attended a reunion concert of Glass Harp in May (2014) and spent time with the guys reminiscing.

Occasionally I meet Eric Carmen at my favorite cigar shop. He started with The Raspberries and became a hit solo artist. Carmen, well known for the recording "All by Myself," and "Hungry Eyes" was played in the movie "Dirty Dancing."

Three special local musicians in my Cleveland life have been: Maceo Noisette (guitar), Steve Gordon (guitar) and David McDougald (bass). Northeast Ohio is ripe with excellent musicians. Maceo, was a solid guitar man who had a friendly personality. He was a charmer and died young.

Steve is an extraordinary bluesman who I would compare to any guitarist in the last thirty years. Dreadlock Dave is one of the finest bass players and a serious student of the bass.

I spent thirteen years being the only Slovak/Italian in a Slovenian band. The Tony Klepec Orchestra was a popular ethnic group from Girard, Ohio. Tony played button box, a chromatic instrument similar to the accordion. He is one the best. Born in Slovenia, he speaks broken English which is overshadowed by a friendly, outgoing personality.

His son, George, played drums and fraternal twin brother, Tony, played keyboard and piano accordion. Anna Marie, his youngest child, sang. Andy played clarinet and saxophone and I played electric bass.

After a few years, Andy left the group and Norm, a phenomenal musician who also played flute, came aboard. Occasionally, Marion, a happy-go-lucky German, played the tuba. I was recruited into the band after an audition.

I sang American tunes and rock and roll. I was also asked to front the group since I had a big personality and being a jovial fat guy in a polka band fit. Finally, I could sing in Slovenian although I didn't understand the language.

In the ethnic world of Eastern Europeans, there are picnic and campgrounds throughout the United States. Most ethnic people, even though American citizens, maintain a close relationship with the old country. The weekends at these facilities are filled with music, dancing, good food, plenty of beer, wine and spirits.

The one complaint commonly heard at these facilities, no matter the ethnic sector, is that prices are too high. Most ethnics are frugal and all are hard workers. They also speak in their native tongue.

We traveled, usually on weekends, to Pennsylvania, Illinois, Michigan and New York. Canada was a regular stop. We did a show in El Paso, Texas. It was a dream come true. Tony's friend, Serene, was with General Motors in Texas. He had a friend who was involved in putting together a three-day festival that was sponsored by the National Park Service.

The event was to be held at the Chamizal National Memorial on the border of Mexico. One of the groups that was booked cancelled at the last minute and we were added. All expenses were covered and we were well paid.

There were about twenty acts. Most were known nationally and many could be heard on National Public Radio (NPR). It turned out to be quite an experience and a lot of fun.

The main show featured a Mexican vocalist and performer, La-Perla, who was famous in that part of the country. She would close out the festivities on the last night and her appearance was broadcast live via satellite on NPR Radio. We were scheduled to appear before her but not included in the radio feed. The Tony Klepec Orchestra did a warm-up act for a star headliner.

La-Perla was middle aged, beautiful, friendly, charismatic and a pleasure to meet. After the show she mingled with her fans, signed autographs and posed for pictures. She wasn't "Hollywood."

Our group was treated like stars. The park was huge and we appeared in about eight venues over three days. Our equipment was transported by a team of roadies and we were driven in golf carts to each performance. Between shows I had an opportunity to watch some of the other acts.

On the final night there was a party for all the acts. It was informal and everyone was welcomed to perform. I heard some of the best music ever at that get together.

A Mexican group of singers took a small stage and sang a beautiful song acappella. Their young lead vocalist held a note longer than I have ever heard and had a smooth melodic voice. It was a great night to be a musician.

We appeared with "polka king" Frank Yankovic. He was old and over the hill but loved to perform and had personality.

We appeared in shows with Walter Ostanek, known as Canada's polka king. Tony and Walter are friends and would periodically exchange CDs they'd recorded. Walter once asked Tony who is playing bass on his CD. Tony said Nick Timcisko. He was impressed with the steadiness and simplicity of my playing. I took it as a compliment and was honored.

We did a variety of ethnic music with a focus on Slovenian. We also played German, Croatian, Slovak and some Italian tunes. Every now and again, I got to do some good old rock and roll.

It was a great run and I enjoyed watching Tony's children mature, marry and start families. We remain in contact. He takes tours to Slovenia, Germany and the Alps and always asks me to consider a trip. Someday I'll do it.

Hawaii

If you have never visited Hawaii, it is the closest thing to paradise. Do yourself a favor and make this a "must see" visit. If I were younger, I may have remained there for the rest of my life.

Carol and I married on a cold, snowy but beautiful Saturday on February 10, 1968. I was attending college and went to school on Monday and never had a honeymoon.

Going to Hawaii was a dream and in 2013, forty-five years later, the time arrived. It would be a three week visit. I booked everything and developed an itinerary.

On Thanksgiving, the flight departed from a cold, snowy Cleveland for a twelve-hour flight to Honolulu and arrived at three in the afternoon. Thanks to tailwinds, we landed an hour early. The transport to the hotel finally arrived and we checked in at five.

The Hilton Waikiki Village is a palatial, beautiful but typical reservation designed to keep you and your cash in their pocket. Shops, businesses and restaurants were everywhere. They were remodeling. We registered and were escorted by the bellman to the twenty-five story Tara Tower. Our upgraded room faced the Pacific Ocean and we started our experience in "tip" city.

Everyone has their hand out. However, it is different from New York City, Boston or Chicago where everyone demands a tip; usually with a scowl on their face. In Hawaii, they have the aloha spirit. Respect our land, ocean, culture and we will love you, brother and sister, uncle and auntie or cousin.

Waikiki Beach is like Hollywood's Rodeo Drive.

I called my friend, Glenn who owns Cruizin' Hawaii, a motorcycle rental company. I met Glenn during a reunion concert of my band, The Del Rays, in 1992 at the Struthers Field House. Glenn is an accomplished bass player and sound engineer.

He was a friend of my drummer, Bruce, and is tall, quiet, laid-back, easy going and methodical. We made him an honorary member of the band for one night of service. His wife, Chris, is a tall beauty.

Both are bikers so when they vacationed they always rented from Cruisin' Hawaii. Glenn jokingly told the owner if he ever needed a mechanic to call him. About seven years ago on their eighteenth trip, the owner offered him a job. They have no children and Glenn has always been self-employed, doing mechanical work, restoring Corvettes and repairing and rebuilding motorcycles.

He moved into a small apartment above the business and started his new endeavor. Chris remained in Youngstown, employed at Youngstown State

University. The couple was together in soul and spirit but living 5000 miles apart. Five years ago Glenn purchased the business and Chris recently retired. It's a beautiful story.

He met us in the lobby of the Hilton Hawaiian Village and we dined at Cheeseburger Paradise on Lewers Street. It is across from the Wyndham, where we would stay in a few days. Later I smoked a fine cigar at the hotel in a secluded spot. There is no smoking permitted on the beach or within twenty feet of a building but we were on our honeymoon.

Very early Friday morning I jumped out of bed and found the only 24-hour coffee shop, the Wialana near the Hawaiian Village. The restaurant is a throwback stuck in the 1960s. They only charged $2.10 for all you want coffee, and everything on the menu looked reasonably priced. You've been places that deserve a second look.

By nine we were having breakfast at the hotel, facing the Pacific Ocean. Carol ordered fried eggs, toast, bacon, home fries and juice. I had an omelet and coffee. The bill was $70. We did some exploring after I took some Advil to alleviate the pain in my wallet. Remember, this is our belated honeymoon.

Waikiki Beach is congested with high-priced stores: Louis Vuitton, Tiffany's, Coldstone Creamery (pricey, pricey, pricey). They will be demolishing the

International Market Center, a well-known spot, to build a Saks Fifth Avenue. The locals are up in arms but that's progress. Think of how many places you visited that are gone.

Later we caught a bus in front of the Ilikai Hotel, adjacent to the Hilton, for a snorkeling trip to Hanauma Bay. Carol was on the cell phone with her brother who was giving her a down by down description of the Ohio State-Michigan football game. You know how important sports can be. Ohio State pulled out a narrow victory and a scream went up from the lobby of the Ilikai. Now Ohio State will play Michigan State for the Big Ten championship and hopefully a trip to the Rose Bowl in Pasadena, California.

The bay was picturesque. I snorkeled while Carol sunbathed. They don't rent towels so we purchased one for thirty dollars. It was gray and windy but we saw fish, coral, and sea turtles. It was fun. We returned to the hotel, stored our luggage and did some exploring.

A taxi drove us to the Wyndham where we expected to relax for a week at a condo. The owner cancelled our reservation. By six we finally had a unit but the lanai (balcony) faced the parking deck which was unacceptable. I demanded a change.

Sunday we had an all-day bus tour of Oahu and the folks at the complex promised to get things worked out. We were then moved to a larger unit which had three lanais (balconies) and was elegant. The largest faced the ocean and it was a fabulous stay.

Have you ever visited a "Coldstone Creamery" ice cream store? For a $2 tip they sang us a song "We ain't no Baskin Robins." The product was delicious.

I went for an early morning walk and found the Duke Pau Kohonamoku statue. Duke introduced surfing to California and Australia. He is a god and people place leis on his outstretched arms. Hawaiian's had many gods and Pele, the god of fire, is credited with creating the Islands.

I passed a police station and spoke to a cop who reviewed the smoking laws with me. He did not tell me about the cell phone laws and one day I was stopped. You are not permitted to talk on a cell phone while driving. Luckily, I got a warning.

The park with Duke's statue is filled with homeless people who sleep there. One morning, I struck up a conversation with a Hawaiian in his sixties who was picking up trash. He did it because it he loved the island and said it would have pleased his father.

Sunday we took the "All of Oahu" bus tour. It rained so being on a bus was a blessing. We saw many sites and our guide explained a lot about

Hawaii and its history. The clouds hung low but we had a great time. In the evening I walked back to Duke's statue and met five more homeless men. One was a Christian who spoke about Jesus. Another fellow knew Eddie Akai, a famous surfer who drowned while attempting to save folks from an overturned canoe.

Visiting the sacred monuments at Pearl Harbor was intense and emotional and Monday the tour started with a self-guided audio program which cited some interesting facts about the attack by the Japanese on December 7, 1941. We took a ferry to the USS Arizona Memorial and saw oil still leaking from the sunken vessel, about two quarts a day. It will continue for at least 75 years and it was a somber visit.

On Tuesday we rented a car and took the movie tour at the Kualoa Ranch. The property is huge and the sights are many. In the afternoon we visited The Point, a beautiful view of the Pacific, then drove to the Polynesian Cultural Center for a luau. It was not authentic but the Brigham Young University students in costume put on a good show.

Wednesday, it was off to the North Shore to snorkel and Kayak. We met Uncle Bryan, a wealthy 62-year-old surfer. He was a character and offered me snorkeling gear for free. His thirty-five foot power boat was docked in the nearby harbor. We got an up-close look at his cruiser and his recently built home.

He insisted on giving me a surfer poster and a cap that said, "Just passing through." We became friends. I declined the kayaking because the seating was low for my titanium hips. We drove toward Honolulu and watched professional surfing at Sunset Bay.

Turtle Bay is a beautiful park with a hotel, condo complex and quite a view. After snorkeling I met Fred, a chef who owns Ola, an upscale restaurant on the beach. We reviewed his menu and agreed to come for dinner on Friday. Fresh sea food is the norm.

Thursday was beach time and then a dinner cruise on the Makani catamaran. We had a great taxi ride from our condo with Mr. Lee. He was having wife issues and very funny as he complained about his spouse. The cruise was a nice two hours on the ocean. We laughed about Mr. Lee for a week.

Friday it was back to Pearl Harbor. A self-guided tour of the submarine USS Bowfin and the USS Missouri is not to be missed. We drove to Ola for dinner. I was unable to make a reservation but hoped we could be seated for dinner.

The owner wasn't in but the manager and staff were friendly and this became a wonderful experience.

Chris, our waiter, said that Fred was called to his other location and was being contacted. He said to "comp" us on any appetizer. I had already ordered a $25 seafood sampler so it was on the house.

Carol had a delicious steak and I ordered fresh scallops. The atmosphere and storybook the view of the Pacific Ocean is breathtaking. The staff liked the two honeymooners that we were and decided to give us an employee discount. The bill for a $150 meal was $46. I left our waiter a big tip. It was slow getting back but another wonderful day in paradise.

Saturday morning we checked out of the condo and planned to fly Island Air to Maui. Their prop planes flew low so we would have a good view of the islands. I paid an extra $60 so that we could get to our condo before the start of the Ohio State-Michigan State game. After OSU lost, we went to Cheeseburgers in Paradise on historic Front Street in Lahina. We are saddened by the loss but there are no unhappy days in Hawaii.

Sunday we toured Front Street in a white Mustang convertible and I found Sir Winfred's, a cigar store. That evening there was the Old Lahina, authentic Polynesian luau. I stayed as the roasted pig was being removed from the underground pit called an imu. The cooks handed me a taste of the freshly cooked pork. Delicious!

We enjoyed the show by a Hawaiian band that had guitar, ukulele, string bass and steel guitar. The singing was heavenly and we had a last dance when the three-hour spectacle ended.

Monday, Francine, who I met in Waikiki Beach, invited us to lunch. Marco's Restaurant was neat and served delicious chicken parmesan and fish. We walked to a local business to try shave ice. It was like eating flavored snow. Nearby was the starting point of the dangerous thirty-mile Road to Hana.

Tuesday's early morning cruise with the Pacific Whale Society, an environmental group, introduced us to whales and large schools of dolphin. We strolled along historic Front Street and a lady enticed us into having lunch at Fleetwood's by offering us a free appetizer. A hamburger, fries and fish and chips hit the spot. We had a beautiful view of the ocean from the rooftop and the food was great.

On the way out I learned that it is owned by Mick Fleetwood, the drummer and leader of the group Fleetwood Mac. That made it special. We were told that Mick could be appearing that evening and later learned he did show up. Unfortunately, we didn't make it back.

Wednesday, I discovered we were near the Ritz Carlton. It was palatial and rooms are up to $2500 a night. I took pictures as we strolled around the gorgeous property and view of the ocean. Even though we were not staying at the hotel we were treated like royalty.

Thursday morning I went out for coffee early in the morning and stumbled into Java Jazz. FarZad, the owner, is Iranian and a defender of America. He plays guitar and spoke three languages. I purchased his CD but missed the jazz group which performs there on Wednesdays. Later, I came for dinner and listened to an excellent vocalist who sang original songs and some James Taylor tunes.

The Road to Hana is a challenging and dangerous three-hour drive. We took a picnic lunch and were guided by a self-directed CD to many stops beside the road. Carol was petrified and me, in my glory!

That evening after dinner at Java Jazz, I met Irish Mick and his friend from England. I stopped at a nearby beach where I again met Mick, his friend and Roger who was 71 years old. They were sharing beer and called themselves the Three Stooges.

Friday it was Front Street and Coldstone ice cream. Carol went to the adjacent mall and I walked to Sir Wilfred's and purchased a Big Kahuna box of cigars. We returned to our beautiful, newly remodeled condo at 5.

I planned to have dinner at Java Jazz where they had a fresh fish, scallops and shrimp plate on the menu.

Carol doesn't eat fish and had me go through the drive-in at McDonalds and drop her off at the condo to rest. I dined alone.

The meal was great and I asked about dessert. Tammy, my server, suggested bread pudding which I had never eaten. Yummy! I stopped at the park where I had met the Three Stooges. Roger was there and Mick soon showed up. We took turns philosophizing and then I headed home.

I was told by a local that homeless people get by in Hawaii very easily. The weather is perfect, so you can make do without a place. All beaches are public and most have showers to rinse off sea water. Many mornings I saw men washing their hair with soap and realized they were homeless taking their showers.

Rest rooms with sinks, commodes and toilet paper are everywhere. Food is all you need. We purchased $35 worth of items in a grocery store for $85. Gasoline was $3.85 a gallon and milk is expensive.

Later, I relaxed in a hot tub with a couple from British Columbia and a man and his Japanese wife. One fellow from Israel spoke about the army and makeup of the country: Palestinians, Christians and Muslim. He said the Sunnis and Shiites are killing each other over religious differences.

We spoke of the beauty of Hawaii and friendliness of the people. It's expensive but locals find a way to get by. Peace and tranquility are the focus.

Saturday, the stay at the condo was over. Carol cooked a breakfast feast: eggs, bacon, home fried potatoes, Hawaiian bread with butter, pineapple, orange juice and Kona coffee before we departed.

We stopped by Java Jazz enroute to the airport and our flight to Hawaii. We were scheduled to depart at noon on the last direct flight to the big island. We planned to take a helicopter tour at three.

Whenever I travel by air I always mention I have two hips made of titanium. The new high-tech scanners are great but the older ones trigger an alarm. Well, guess what? It was old technology.

The TSA officer pats me down three times, feels me up two more times and tells me to have a seat. He walks away for twenty minutes and finally says I'm cleared. We missed our direct flight to Hilo by three minutes. Now we will arrive at 7. We pick up our rental car and check into the Volcano Forest Inn at 8 in the evening, so no helicopter.

The inn is an old bed and breakfast, situated on a desolate road, near the Volcano National Park. Carlos, the innkeeper, was there to greet us. He is a jolly man with personality. He arranged to become the innkeeper and divorced his wife who decided paradise wasn't for her. He told us the rules, no shoes allowed, led us to our spacious room and said, "Good night."

Sunday I was still awake at 2 am so I sat on the front porch and had a cigar. We plan to drive through the Volcano National Park in a few hours and then around the island. It's a vast wasteland.

On the way we lunch at Shaka's, a quaint, dumpy bar located on the southernmost point of the US. I met the owner and enjoyed tasty fresh fish.

On the drive to Hilo, we stop at a black sand beach and watch three huge sea turtles sunning themselves. We reach Kona at nine and locate Uncle Billy's Hotel. We are definitely in the 1950s. The room is plain but the view is breathtaking.

Monday morning, I meet the front desk manager and purchase a paper. On the way out, we take photos and have a delicious breakfast. We drive to the Hilo Airport and return our rental car. The security check goes smoothly and we arrive in Honolulu at eleven where we pick up a Chevrolet Impala. Its solid black, Carol's least favorite color, but the trunk is huge and it is roomy.

There is a traffic jam in Waikiki and we finally get to Cruisin' Hawaii and surprise Glenn and his wife. After chatting and making dinner plans, we check into the Ilikai Hotel. The AAA package we bought includes parking ($35 per day, valet parking) and in-out privileges. We'll drop the car at the airport when we depart Tuesday morning.

Wayne, our bellman, escorts us to our room but it's not the view I requested so we move. The new room has a breathtaking view of the private marina where the opening shot of the TV program "Gilligan's Island" was filmed and the Pacific ocean.

Tonight we take Glenn and Chris to dinner and asked them to choose a place. We get some sun and relax on the beach. Carol is not a water person and the ocean has not been past her knees. She walks the beach with the surf under her feet.

Glenn and Chris arrive and we watch a magnificent sunset which I photograph, then head off to dinner. Our friends are tall and the roomy Impala is a blessing. Glenn drives and serves as tour guide, pointing out many interesting sights. We see the pool where Johnny Weismuiller and Duke Kohonomoku trained for the 1924 Olympic swimming competition. It's in disarray and the locals want to save the historic pool but no money has been raised. Remember Tarzan?

We pass a wealthy gated neighborhood and Glenn mentions a Japanese businessman purchased some properties and opened art galleries filled with garish art and sculptures. He was jailed for fraud and the property, included the artworks, was auctioned off.

We pass the zoo and arrive at the Star Restaurant which overlooks a small bay and order dinner. Chris wants to buy or leave the tip but I told them the next time. It was a wonderful having a meal with our good friends. Tomorrow we leave paradise.

I take a stroll in the evening and find a wooden deck chair next to some beautiful plants on the hotel patio along the ocean. I light my OpusX cigar made by Fuente. It is slow burning and tasty. I relax then review our Hawaiian dream honeymoon in my mind. Thank you, Lord, for all You have provided. Tomorrow evening it is back to Chagrin Falls, Ohio.

Tuesday I walk to the Wialana, my favorite place at 4 a.m. The coffee is great and I have a piece of plain New York cheesecake. The service and attitude of the people is fantastic and food is fresh and reasonably priced.

I speak to the manager who graduated from Purdue. We talk about Ohio State, Bob Knight and things in general. At 5 a.m., I go back to the Ilikai. I do some writing as I wait for the dawn and then we go to Magic Beach, a public park in the Ala Moana National Park. The sand is clean and smooth.

Our original bellman, Wayne, arrives to take our luggage and I give him an extra tip. He was very pleasant as were most of the staff people we met throughout our travels in Hawaii. We will make a short drive to the Honolulu Airport but make a last stop at Glenn and Chris's apartment.

Carol and Glenn, who have much in common, start talking about motorcycles. Carol still recalls a scary ride on a Moped scooter when she was a teen. Glenn said she didn't have the right driver. The next thing I know, Carol puts on a helmet. I remind Glenn that Carol is an older woman and if he has any thoughts of stealing my honey, I will come looking for them.

They are off for a ride on a beautiful Triumph motorcycle to Diamond Head and will return when Carol has had enough, and they return in twenty minutes. Chris walks down when they rerun and we share our goodbyes.

For 17 years, their business was housed in a 450-square-foot storefront below their apartment The rent was $5000 a month. Insurance on bikes, no matter what size is $130 a month per bike. Friends, we are talking a lot of overhead to stay afloat. Glenn has made cuts but plans to moves the business in a few months.

It is difficult to depart from what is truly paradise on earth. The aloha spirit is about peace, tranquility and being one with all and God. One Hawaiian commented that money was "evil." The love of it surely is the downfall of many.

We land in Newark and spent three hours in New Jersey. Our first encounter on the mainland, a Latino women with a child screaming, cursing and acting like a fool. It was a contrast to Honolulu. Most people were walking around with somber and sour looks. Our flight to Cleveland was on time. It is cold but sunny.

On February 10, 2014, we celebrated 46 years of marriage. On February 21, I turned 70 years of age. The time has flown by and our hair is graying but our love for each other, our children, grandchildren and each other is strong. I'm past the fourth quarter of life and realize I can't change yesterday and there may be no tomorrow. Make today the best day ever.

No ocean breeze, no ocean, no beautiful sun, no 82 degrees...we are back in Chagrin Falls, Ohio. It's a rainy day and 50 degrees, warm for winter. The snow is melting. Carol has already run the washer many times and, of course, the vacuum cleaner is no longer lonely. The dirty floor is driving her crazy and nearly all of our travel items are in their proper place.

When you think about the places you've visited or seen, what kind of impact did the experience have?

I must express a final thought which was provided to me at one of the hotels we frequented. I am a changed man.

The Aloha Spirit

We believe that the most important gift we can give our guests is that feeling of Aloha. "Aloha Spirit" is the coordination of mind and heart...it's within you. You must think and emote good feelings to others.

A   stands for AKHAI, meaning kindness, to be expressed with tenderness.

L   stands for LOKAHI, meaning unity, to be expressed with harmony.

O   stands for OLU'OLU, meaning agreeable, to be expressed with pleasantness.

H   stands for HA'AHA'A, meaning humility, to be expressed with modesty.

A   stands for AHONUI, meaning patience, to be expressed with perseverance

By Pilahi Paki

Finish

On June 29, 2013, I visited the Apple Store in Legacy Village to buy my first Apple computer product, a MacBook Air (MBA). I bought the works. I was told to bring my HP Slimline tower in the next day to have my documents transferred.

I arrived at 10 with high expectations, only to be told the store was relocating the next day to Eton Square and I would need to return. I was irritated.

Saturday, I arrived at the new location and was escorted in as the first customer. It proved to be one of the most exciting days of my life. The Apple culture was in full force. There was magic in the air. The associates whooped and hollered as people entered. It truly was a grand opening. I felt chills as I led the charge into the store.

A total focus on the customer dominated the day. My dismay was relieved by a focus on me and my issues. Professionalism was the order of the day.

By my third visit to the store, I became an Apple fan to the core. I learned "one-on-one" meant individual tutoring by an associate and support from all the geniuses that occupy the back office. I was ecstatic. I now understand what makes Apple a great company. Beside excellent products the attention I received was appreciated.

I can't stop talking about Apple products, the culture and the employees dedicated to sharing their skill. I am learning how to use my Mac.

I now own an iPhone even though I loved my antiquated flip phone. I use many features and it is a great camera. I went to Apple school for an overview of the product but have more to learn.

The only thing constant is change and it comes fast.

The nanny state will eventually cause the demise of many things including cigar shops. Federal laws have been passed to control: health care, guns, food, speech and there is a move to limit our rights. For example, the FDA is attempting to bring all tobacco under its control. There is a negative attitude toward smokers and pressure is being applied.

I hope you enjoyed this book and found it informing and relative. Life has changed. Today evil is being presented as good and good as evil. We are in a crisis, politically. Music has changed. The airwaves are filled with obscene and horrible lyrics. The venues that presented opportunities for many musicians are gone.

Movies, TV and videos are violent and morally low. Animals may soon have more rights than people. Americans are becoming an entitlement society. Credit has enabled instant gratification and placed many in bondage.

We are racing toward Communism, even though it has failed everywhere. Lt. General Russel Honore' in the second Gulf War said, "Don't get stuck on stupid." Today, many are stuck.

I pray that our Constitution survives and that we the people wake up and come back to life. Grandma Wasko always said, "You don't get something for nothing."

"Little things console us because little things afflict us."

Blaise Pascal

TO CATHOLIC BELIEVERS AND OTHERS: YOU CAN BE SURE OF HEAVEN

Raised Catholic (Byzantine), I was in a monastery, seminary, and might have been a priest.

*"But as many as received Him, He gave them power to be made the sons of God, to them that believed in His name" (John 1:12).

*"For God so loved the world as to give His only begotten Son, that whosoever believeth in Him may not perish, but may have life everlasting" (John 3:16).

*"Amen, Amen, I say unto you that he who heareth My Word, and believith Him that sent Me, hath life everlasting; and cometh not into judgment, but is passed from death to life" (John 5:24).

*"Now this is eternal life; that they may know Thee, the only true God, and Jesus Christ, whom thou has sent" (John 17:3).

*"Christ died for us; much more therefore, being justified by His blood, shall be saved from wrath through Him" (Romans 5:9).

*"For if thou confess with thy mouth the Lord Jesus, and believe in thy heart that God hath raised Him up from the dead, thou shall be saved" (Romans 10:9).

*"For by grace you are saved through faith; and not of yourselves, for it is the gift of God, not of works, that no man may glory" (Ephesians 2:8-9).

*"Whereby He is able also to save forever them that comes to God by Him; always living to make intercession for us" (Hebrews 7:25).

*"And this is the testimony, that God hath given to us eternal life. And this life is in His Son. He that hath the Son hath life. He that hath not the Son hath not life" (1John 5:11-12).

*"Being born again not of corruptible seed, but incorruptible, by the Word of God, who livith and remainith forever" (1Peter 1:23).

*NOTE: All verses are from the Douay (Catholic) version of the Holy Bible.

These 10 passages of Holy Scripture, quoted from three of the apostles, St. Peter, St. John, and St Paul, plainly show that salvation is a gift, is by grace, by which we are saved and have eternal life. How tragic if you lose your soul and spend eternity in hell because you did not learn the truth revealed by God in His Holy Word.

Today, God wants you to knowingly, and willingly, accept, and receive, His Son, the Lord Jesus Christ, as your Personal Savior. NOW, on the authority of God's Word (the Holy Scriptures), pray this prayer: Lord, I acknowledge that I am a sinner. I now repent and turn from sin. I believe that Jesus died to save me, and I now call upon You, in the name of Your son, Jesus Christ, and ask for forgiveness and your saving grace.

Upon this prayer, you start a new life. By praying this prayer, you can have peace and joy such as you have never known. You now know that you will spend eternity in heaven, and now begin a personal relationship with God, through His Son, Jesus Christ, and are empowered by the Holy Ghost (Spirit). God, in His Word says, "Because greater is He who is in you, than he that is in the world." (1John 4:4)

nicktimcisko@aol.com

AFTER THOUGHTS

On August 10, 2014, Comedian and Actor Robin Williams took his life at the age of 63. He was loved by many and respected by all. He suffered from severe depression. This was one of many demons he battled throughout his life.

The world mourned the man who started his career as Mork from Ork on the "Mork and Mindy" television show which was seen from 1978 to 1982. He had a quick mind and was cast from the same mold as Jonathan Winters, the famous comedian.

Genius and fame is a dangerous combination. It is both a blessing and a curse. You're always "on" and usually your worst enemy and critic. You are never good enough and have a tendency to be a perfectionist. Insecurity is a common trait.

No matter what others say, people usually obsess over minor issues. The mind is complex and people are fragile. We all tend to wear a mask.

Having success and things will not buy happiness. Think about Ernest Hemingway, Marilyn Monroe, Del Shannon and now Robin Williams. They all gave much but it was probably never enough in their eyes.

It is sad when you think about how easy it is to stray from things which are important. Friends, family, simple pleasures, relationships and health. None of these things can be purchased and often is taken for granted. We all want to be loved. To have a friend demands you be a friend. True friends are few. Unconditional love is a key to serenity.

In today's fast-paced world, it is a good idea to step back and slow down long enough to take a look at what is really important. Start each day by thanking God for what you have been given.

My hope is that your journey through life has been fulfilling and that you experience joy and peace. In the final analysis, the greatest is love. Know that you have been created for a purpose and are loved by your Creator.

About the Author

I was born in Youngstown, Ohio, adopted and raised Byzantine Catholic. I became an altar boy and spent summer in a monastery. My family hoped I would be a priest. I lived with my maternal grandmother as a child and sang my first song in the third grade.

I played football in high school, learned guitar and started The Del Rays, a popular rock and roll band. I quit college, moved to Washington DC and worked for The C&P of Virginia (AT&T). I returned to college to study Business and Marketing.

I married, was hired by Xerox Corporation and received my BS in BA from Youngstown State University. I was promoted to Rochester, NY, and relocated to Newport News, Virginia where I managed sales to: the Continental Army Command, Fort Monroe, Transportation School, Fort Eustis, Tactical Air Command, Langley Air Force Base and NASA.

I was awakened at a Billy Graham Crusade in Hampton, Virginia which started a journey that continues. I returned to Ohio, was employed by Ohio Bell then became self-employed. I've faced low self-esteem, fear, mental illness, failure, bankruptcy and other challenges.

Today, I'm a businessman, professional musician, writer and happily married. Carol and I have three adult children, eight grandchildren and live in Bainbridge Township, Ohio.

My goal in life is to encourage, serve, listen, love, learn and be where God takes me. I love the USA and enjoy things money can't buy.

8140 Stoney Brook Drive   Chagrin Falls, OH 44023
nicktimcisko@aol.com

Encouragement & Love

www.upinsmokebynick.com

Jeremiah 9:23-24